Q & A's About:

Salvation

By: Only A. Guy

Hard Questions About: Salvation

Published 2012

Published by VIP Ink Publishing

Cover Art and Editing By Whyte Lady Designs L.L.C.

www.onlyaguy.com
www.facebook.com/onlyaguy
www.twitter.com/onlyaguy1

www.vipinkpublishing.com

ISBN 13: 978-0-9847382-8-1
ISBN: 978-0-9847382-8-1

Printed in the USA.

If you like this book here are some others coming out by this author you may find enjoyable as well as educational:

2011

HARD QUESTIONS ABOUT GOD
HARD QUESTIONS ABOUT JESUS
THE BOOK OF PRAYERS

2012

HARD QUESTIONS ABOUT THE HOLY SPIRIT
HARD QUESTIONS ABOUT HEAVEN AND HELL
HARD QUESTIONS ABOUT ANGELS AND DEMONS
HARD QUESTIONS ABOUT SALVATION
HOPE IN A LOST AND FALLEN WORLD

2013

HARD QUESTIONS ABOUT THE END TIMES
HARD QUESTIONS ABOUT CHRISTIANITY
HARD QUESTIONS ABOUT CREATION
HARD QUESTIONS ABOUT HUMANITY

2014

HARD QUESTIONS ABOUT LIFE'S DECISIONS
HARD QUESTIONS ABOUT CULTS AND RELIGIONS
HARD QUESTIONS ABOUT FALSE DOCTRINE
HARD QUESTIONS ABOUT PRAYER
HARD QUESTIONS ABOUT SIN

Question: "What is salvation? What is the Christian doctrine of salvation?"

Salvation is deliverance from danger or suffering. To save is to deliver or protect. The word carries the idea of victory, health, or preservation. Sometimes, the Bible uses the words saved or salvation to refer to temporal, physical deliverance, such as Paul's deliverance from prison *(Philippians 1:19)*. More often, the word salvation concerns an eternal, spiritual deliverance. When Paul told the Philippian jailer what he must do to be saved, he was referring to the jailer's eternal destiny *(Acts 16:30-31)*. Jesus equated being saved with entering the kingdom of God *(Matthew 19:24-25)*.

- **What are we saved from?** In the Christian doctrine of salvation, we are saved from "wrath"; that is, from God's judgment of sin *(Romans 5:9; 1 Thessalonians 5:9)*. Our sin has separated us from God, and the consequence of sin is death *(Romans 6:23)*. Biblical salvation refers to our deliverance from the consequence of sin and therefore involves the removal of sin.
- **Who does the saving?** Only God can remove sin and deliver us from sin's penalty *(2 Timothy 1:9; Titus 3:5)*.
- **How does God save?** In the Christian doctrine of salvation, God has rescued us through Christ *(John 3:17)*. Specifically, it was Jesus' death on the cross and subsequent resurrection that achieved our salvation *(Romans 5:10; Ephesians 1:7)*. Scripture is clear that salvation is the gracious, undeserved gift of God *(Ephesians 2:5, 8)* and is only available through faith in Jesus Christ *(Acts 4:12)*.
- **How do we receive salvation?** We are saved by faith. First, we must hear the gospel, the good news of Jesus' death and resurrection *(Ephesians 1:13)*. Then, we must believe and fully trust the Lord Jesus *(Romans 1:16)*. This involves repentance, a changing of mind about sin and Christ *(Acts 3:19)*, and calling on the name of the Lord *(Romans 10:9-10, 13)*.

A definition of the Christian doctrine of salvation would be "The spiritual, eternal deliverance which God immediately grants to those who accept His conditions of repentance and faith in the Lord Jesus." Salvation is available in Jesus alone *(John 14:6; Acts 4:12)*, and is dependent on God alone for provision, assurance, and security.

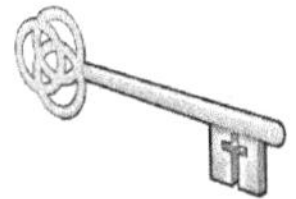

Question: "What is the plan of salvation/way of salvation?"

Are you hungry? Not physically hungry, but do you have a hunger for something more in life? Is there something deep inside you that never seems to be satisfied? If so, Jesus is the way! Jesus said, *"I am the bread of life. He who comes to me will never go hungry, and he who believes in me will never be thirsty" (John 6:35).*

Are you confused? Can you never seem to find a path or purpose in life? Does it seem like someone has turned out the lights and you cannot find the switch? If so, Jesus is the way! Jesus proclaimed, *"I am the light of the world. Whoever follows me will never walk in darkness, but will have the light of life" (John 8:12).*

Do you ever feel like you are locked out of life? Have you tried so many doors, only to find that what is behind them is empty and meaningless? Are you looking for an entrance into a fulfilling life? If so, Jesus is the way! Jesus declared, *"I am the gate; whoever enters through me will be saved. He will come in and go out, and find pasture" (John 10:9).*

Do other people always let you down? Have your relationships been shallow and empty? Does it seem like everyone is trying to take advantage of you? If so, Jesus is the way! Jesus said, *"I am the good shepherd. The good shepherd lays down his life for the sheep...I am the good shepherd; I know my sheep and my sheep know me" (John 10:11, 14).*

Do you wonder what happens after this life? Are you tired of living your life for things that only rot or rust? Do you sometimes doubt whether life has any meaning? Do you want to live after you die? If so, Jesus is the way! Jesus declared, *"I am the resurrection and the life. He who believes in me will live, even though he dies; and whoever lives and believes in me will never die" (John 11:25-26).*

What is the way? What is the truth? What is the life? Jesus answered, *"I am the way and the truth and the life. No one comes to the Father except through me" (John 14:6).*

The hunger that you feel is a spiritual hunger, and can only be filled by Jesus. Jesus is the only one who can lift the darkness. Jesus is the gate to a satisfying life. Jesus is the friend and shepherd that you have been looking for. Jesus is the life - in this world and the next. Jesus is the way of salvation!

The reason you feel hungry, the reason you seem to be lost in darkness, the reason you can't find meaning in life, is that you are separated from God. The Bible tells us that we have all sinned, and are therefore separated from God *(Ecclesiastes 7:20; Romans 3:23)*. The void you feel in your heart is God missing from your life. We were created to have a relationship with God. Because of our sin, we are separated from that relationship. Even worse, our sin will cause us to be separated from God for all of eternity, this life and the next *(Romans 6:23; John 3:36)*.

How can this problem be solved? Jesus is the way! Jesus took our sin upon Himself *(2 Corinthians 5:21)*. Jesus died in our place *(Romans 5:8)*, taking the punishment that we deserve. Three days later, Jesus rose from the dead, proving His victory over sin and death *(Romans 6:4-5)*. Why did He do it? Jesus answered that question Himself, *"Greater love has no one than this, that he lay down his life for his friends" (John 15:13)*. Jesus died so that we could live. If we place our faith in Jesus, trusting His death as the payment for our sins - all of our sins are forgiven and washed away. We will then have our spiritual hunger satisfied. The lights will be turned on. We will have access to a fulfilling life. We will know our true best friend and good shepherd. We will know that we will have life after we die - a resurrected life in heaven for eternity with Jesus!

"For God so loved the world that He gave His one and only Son, that whoever believes in Him shall not perish but have eternal life" (John 3:16).

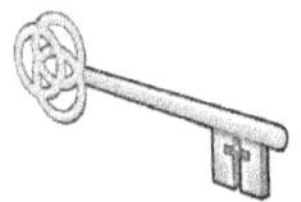

Question: "What is the prayer of salvation?"

Many people ask, "Is there a prayer I can pray that will result in my salvation?" When considering this question, it is important to remember that salvation is not received by reciting a prayer or uttering certain words. The Bible nowhere records a person receiving salvation by a prayer. Saying a prayer is not the Biblical way of salvation.

The Biblical method of salvation is believing in Jesus. *John 3:16* tells us, *"For God so loved the world that He gave His one and only Son, that whoever believes in Him shall not perish but have eternal life."* Salvation is gained by faith *(Ephesians 2:8)*, by receiving Jesus as Savior *(John 1:12)*, by fully trusting Jesus alone *(John 14:6; Acts 4:12).* Not by reciting a prayer.

The Biblical message of salvation is simple and clear, and amazing at the same time. We have all committed sin against God *(Romans 3:23).* There is no one who has lived an entire life without sinning *(Ecclesiastes 7:20)*. Because of our sin, we have earned judgment from God *(Romans 6:23)*, and that judgment is physical death followed by spiritual death. Because of our sin and its deserved punishment, there is nothing we can do on our own to make ourselves right with God. As a result of His love for us, God became a human being in the Person of Jesus Christ. Jesus lived a perfect life and always taught the truth. However, humanity rejected Jesus and put Him to death by crucifying Him. Through that horrible act, though, Jesus died in our place. Jesus took the burden and judgment of sin on Himself, and died for us *(2 Corinthians 5:21)*. Jesus was then resurrected *(1 Corinthians 15)*, proving that His payment for sin was sufficient and that He had overcome sin and death. As a result of Jesus' sacrifice, God offers us salvation as a gift. God calls us all to change our minds about Jesus *(Acts 17:30)*, and to receive Him as the full payment of our sins *(1 John 2:2)*. Salvation is gained by receiving the gift God offers us, not by praying a prayer.

Now, that does not mean prayer cannot be involved in receiving salvation. If you understand the Gospel, believe it to be true, and have accepted Jesus as your salvation then it is good and appropriate to express this faith to God in prayer. Communicating with God through prayer can be a way of progressing from accepting facts about Jesus to be true, to fully trusting in Jesus as Savior. Prayer can be connected to the act of placing your faith in Jesus alone for salvation.

Again, though, it is crucially important that you do not base your salvation on having said a prayer. Reciting a prayer cannot save you! If you want to receive the salvation that is available through Jesus, place your faith in Him. Fully trust His death as the sufficient sacrifice for your sins. Completely rely on Him alone as your Savior. That is the Biblical method of salvation. If you have received Jesus as your Savior, by all means, say a prayer to God. Tell God how thankful you are for Jesus.

Offer praise to God for His love and sacrifice. Thank Jesus for dying for your sins and providing salvation for you. That is the Biblical connection between salvation and prayer!

Question: "What are the steps to salvation?"

"In [Jesus] we have redemption through His blood, the forgiveness of sins, according to the riches of His grace" (Ephesians 1:7).

Giving steps to salvation can be misleading because it implies that a person can work his way to heaven by completing "steps." As the above verse says, salvation is by His grace; we cannot earn it *(Titus 3:5)*. Being dead in sin, an unbeliever doesn't have the capacity to love God *(Ephesians 2:1)*.

Thankfully, *"while we were yet sinners" (Romans 5:8)*, God redeemed us. Redemption is paying the price to loose from bondage. By sacrificing His Son on the cross, God paid the price for sin (which is death), freeing believers from sin's oppression. By resurrecting Christ from the grave, God proved the sacrifice was effective, giving the Lord Jesus authority to rule and intercede at His right hand *(Romans 4:25; Mark 16:19)*.

Although we cannot merit heaven by taking steps to salvation, we are called to respond to Christ's redemption with repentance and faith. Even that response is a gift from God *(Ephesians 2:8-9)*. Thus, the question is correctly worded, *"What are God's steps to salvation of sinners?"* He did it all through Christ!

"For all have sinned and fall short of the glory of God, being justified [declared righteous/not guilty] as a gift by His grace through the redemption which is in Christ Jesus; . . . Where then is boasting? It is excluded. By what kind of law? Of works? No, but by a law of faith. For we maintain that a man is justified by faith apart from works of the Law" (Romans 3:23-24; 27-29).

The next question is, "What should be our response, by God's grace, to Christ's death and resurrection? Let's review the following three responses. Discern whether you need to respond to God's grace to be saved from sin and its sentence of hell.

Steps to Salvation/Response to Christ's Redemption

- **Recognize need:** Before receiving Jesus as Savior, you must understand why you need a Savior. Most people think if they live a law-abiding life, they deserve heaven. The problem is their definition of law-abiding. On Judgment Day after death, we won't stand before a fallible, human judge. We will answer to a holy God, who rightly judges our thoughts, words, and actions. God gives His law in the Bible, summarized by the Ten Commandments. Have you kept them? You might be thinking, "Well, I've never murdered anyone." But Jesus revealed the true meaning of the law. He equated hatred with murder *(Matthew 5:21 -22; 1 John 3:15)*. Looking at someone with lust, Jesus taught, was adultery of the heart *(Matthew 5:27-29)*. Besides, all of us have broken the two greatest commands: loving God wholeheartedly and loving others as ourselves *(Matthew 22:37-40)*. By loving possessions more than God and loving ourselves more than others, we have all *"sinned and fall short of the glory of God" (Romans 3:23)*. Are you guilty? *"If we say that we have no sin, we are deceiving ourselves and the truth is not in us" (1 John 1:8)*. The penalty for sin that we all deserve is death, eternal separation from God in hell *(Romans 6:23)*. Do you realize your need for a Savior from sin? That is God's grace in convicting you!
- **Repent of sin:** In believing in Jesus as Savior, you must change your mind. Repentance isn't a "Sorry I got caught" reaction. It is a change of mind, a heartfelt sorrow of how sin grieves God, resulting in turning away from it to Christ who gives the power to overcome sin. You cannot embrace both sin and Christ. Although repentance leads to a change of behavior, it doesn't mean we'll never sin again. But we will have a different attitude toward it. Instead of craving the gratification of sin's enticements, we'll learn to detest it. God changes the lure of sin for the pure desire of delighting in Himself. After convicting us of sin (first response), God's grace gives us the repentant desire to change (second response). Turning from sin, we turn in faith to the only Savior from sin. This trust in Christ's payment for and triumph over sin involves the third response to God's grace.

- **Receive Christ:** For repentant sinners, God provides salvation from the penalty and power of sin through Jesus. Our response must be faith in who Christ is and what He has done. Jesus lived a perfect life for He was God in the flesh; Jesus died a redemptive death for He is the Savior from sin; Jesus resurrected as the Victor over sin and death for He is Lord over all. By God's grace, we repent of sin, trusting Christ as Savior from sin and following Him as Lord of life. We're born again to new life by the Holy Spirit. Thus, He changes our desires to joy in glorifying the Lord.

In conclusion, a person cannot merit heaven through taking certain steps to salvation. Rather, God calls a sinner to respond to Christ's redemption. Even the response of repentance and faith is His grace. Christians have nothing to be proud about; they boast only in the Lord!

"And you were dead in your trespasses and sins, in which you formerly walked according to the course of this world, according to the prince of the power of the air [Satan], of the spirit that is now working in the sons of disobedience. Among them we too all formerly lived in the lusts of our flesh, indulging the desires of the flesh and of the mind, and were by nature children of wrath, even as the rest. But God, being rich in mercy, because of His great love with which He loved us, even when we were dead in our transgressions, made us alive together with Christ (by grace you have been saved), and raised us up with Him, and seated us with Him in the heavenly places in Christ Jesus, so that in the ages to come He might show the surpassing riches of His grace in kindness toward us in Christ Jesus. For by grace you have been saved through faith; and that not of yourselves, it is the gift of God; not as a result of works, so that no one may boast. For we are His workmanship, created in Christ Jesus for good works, which God prepared beforehand so that we would walk in them" (Ephesians 2:1-10).

Note that God saves Christians unto good works. All other religions require earning salvation by good works. Islam, for example, requires keeping the Five Pillars as steps to salvation.

In our pluralistic society, claiming one religion as truth seems arrogant. But God is not confined by men's wishes and beliefs. As sovereign Judge, He could have let the law condemn us, resulting in eternal separation from Him in hell. But in love, God sent Christ to save His own from sin. Glory to God alone! How do you respond?

Question: "Is eternal security Biblical?"

When people come to know Christ as their Savior, they are brought into a relationship with God that guarantees their eternal security. *Jude 24* declares, *"To Him who is able to keep you from falling and to present you before His glorious presence without fault and with great joy."* God's power is able to keep the believer from falling. It is up to Him, not us, to present us before His glorious presence. Our eternal security is a result of God keeping us, not us maintaining our own salvation

The Lord Jesus Christ proclaimed, *"I give them eternal life, and they shall never perish; no one can snatch them out of my hand. My Father, who has given them to me, is greater than all, no one can snatch them out of my Father's hand" (John 10:28-29b).* Both Jesus and the Father have us firmly grasped in their hand. Who could possibly separate us from the grip of both the Father and the Son?

Ephesians 4:30 tells us that believers are *"sealed for the day of redemption."* If believers did not have eternal security, the sealing could not truly be unto the day of redemption, but only to the day of sinning, apostasy, or disbelief. *John 3:15-16* tells us that whoever believes in Jesus Christ will *"have eternal life."* If a person were to be promised eternal life, but then have it taken away, it was never "eternal" to begin with. If eternal security is not true, the promises of eternal life in the Bible would be in error.

The most powerful argument for eternal security is *Romans 8:38-39, "For I am convinced that neither death nor life, neither angels nor demons, neither the present nor the future, nor any powers, neither height nor depth, nor anything else in all creation, will be able to separate us from the love of God that is in Christ Jesus our Lord."* Our eternal security is based on God's love for those whom He has redeemed. Our eternal security is purchased by Christ, promised by the Father, and sealed by the Holy Spirit.

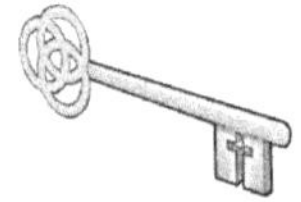

Question: "Is eternal security a "license" to sin?"

The most frequent objection to the doctrine of eternal security is that it supposedly promotes the idea that Christians can live any way that they want to and still be saved. While this is "technically" true that is not the "essence" of eternal security. A person who has truly accepted Jesus Christ as his or her Savior "can" live a sinful life, but he or she will not desire to do so. We must draw a distinction between how a Christian should live and what a person must do in order to receive salvation.

The Bible is abundantly clear that salvation is by grace alone, through faith alone, in Jesus Christ alone *(John 3:16; Ephesians 2:8-9; John 14:6)*. A person is saved by faith and faith alone. The moment a person truly believes in Jesus Christ, he/she is saved and secure in that salvation. It is not that salvation is gained by faith, but then maintained by works. The Apostle Paul addresses this issue in *Galatians 3:3, "Are you so foolish? After beginning with the Spirit, are you now trying to attain your goal by human effort?"* If we are saved by faith, our salvation is also maintained and secured by faith. We cannot earn our own salvation. Therefore, we cannot earn the maintenance of our salvation either. It is God who maintains our salvation *(Jude 24)*. It is God's hand that holds us firmly in His grasp *(John 10:28-29)*. It is God's love that nothing can separate us from *(Romans 8:38-39)*.

Any denial of eternal security is, in its essence, a belief that we must maintain our own salvation by our own good works. This is completely antithetical to salvation by grace. We are saved because of Christ's merits, not our own *(Romans 4:3-8)*. To claim that we must obey God's Word or live a godly life to maintain our salvation is equal to saying that Jesus' death was not sufficient to pay the penalty for our sins. Jesus' death was absolutely sufficient to pay for all of our sins; past, present, and future, *(Romans 5:8; 1 Corinthians 15:3; 2 Corinthians 5:21)*.

So, with all that said, does this mean that a Christian can live any way he/she wants to and still be saved? This is essentially a hypothetical question, because the Bible makes it clear that a true Christian will not live "any way he/she wants to." Christians are new creations *(2 Corinthians 5:17)*. Christians demonstrate the fruit of the Spirit *(Galatians 5:22-23)*, not the acts of the flesh *(Galatians 5:19-21)*. *1 John 3:6-9* clearly states that a true Christian will not live in continual sin. In response to the accusation that grace promotes sin, the Apostle Paul declared, *"What shall we say, then? Shall we go on sinning so that grace may increase? By no means! We died to sin; how can we live in it any longer?" (Romans 6:1-2).*

Eternal security is not a "license" to sin. Rather, it is the security of knowing that God's love is guaranteed for those who trust in Christ. Knowing and understanding God's tremendous gift of salvation accomplishes the opposite of giving a "license" to sin. How could anyone, knowing the price Jesus Christ paid for us, go on to live a life of sin *(Romans 6:15-23)*? How could anyone who understands God's unconditional and guaranteed love for those who believe, take that love and throw it back in God's face? Such a person is demonstrating not that eternal security has given him or her a license to sin, but rather that he or she has not truly experienced salvation through Jesus Christ. *"No one who lives in Him keeps on sinning. No one who continues to sin has either seen Him or known Him" (1 John 3:6).*

Question: "What is Soteriology?"

Soteriology is the study of the doctrine of salvation. Soteriology discusses how Christ's death secures the salvation of those who believe. It helps us to understand the doctrines of redemption, justification, sanctification, propitiation, and the substitutionary atonement. Some common questions in studying Soteriology are:

- **Once saved always saved?** Perhaps the most heart-wrenching fear some believers live with is that we can do something to lose our salvation. But the Bible speaks clearly about the eternality of our salvation and how we are preserved by the One who bought us with His blood.
- **Is salvation by faith alone, or by faith plus works?**
- **Am I saved just by believing in Jesus, or do I have to believe in Jesus and do certain things?**
- **Is baptism required for salvation?**
- **What is baptismal regeneration?** Baptismal regeneration is the belief that a person must be baptized in order to be saved. While baptism is an important step of obedience for a Christian, the Bible

is clear that baptism is not a requirement for salvation.

- **What is repentance and is it necessary for salvation?** Biblical repentance is changing your mind about Jesus Christ and turning to God in faith for salvation *(Acts 3:19)*. Turning from sin is not the definition of repentance, but it is one of the results of genuine, faith-based repentance towards the Lord Jesus Christ.
- *What does it mean to be a born again Christian?* The phrase "born again" literally means "born from above." It is an act of God whereby eternal life is imparted to the person who believes, a spiritual transformation.

Other than Christology, Soteriology is the area where Christianity is the most different from the cults and other world religions. Understanding Biblical Soteriology will help us to know why salvation is by grace alone *(Ephesians 2:8-9)*, through faith alone, in Jesus Christ alone. No other religion bases salvation on faith alone. Soteriology helps us to see why. A clear understanding of our salvation will provide a peace that passes all understanding *(Philippians 4:7)* because we come to know that He who can never fail is the means by which we were saved and the means by which we remain secure in our salvation. If we were responsible to save ourselves and keep ourselves saved, we would fail. Thank God that is not the case!

Titus 3:5-8 is a tremendous summary of Soteriology, *"He saved us, not because of righteous things we had done, but because of His mercy. He saved us through the washing of rebirth and renewal by the Holy Spirit, whom He poured out on us generously through Jesus Christ our Savior, so that, having been justified by His grace, we might become heirs having the hope of eternal life."*

Question: "Got Forgiveness? How do I receive forgiveness from God?"

Acts 13:38 declares, *"Therefore, my brothers, I want you to know that through Jesus the forgiveness of sins is proclaimed to you."*

- **What is forgiveness and why do I need it?** The word "forgive" means to wipe the slate clean, to pardon, to cancel a debt. When we wrong someone, we seek their forgiveness in order for the relationship to be restored. Forgiveness is not granted because a person deserves to be forgiven. No one deserves to be forgiven. Forgiveness is an act of love, mercy, and grace. Forgiveness is a decision to not hold something against another person, despite what they have done to you. The Bible tells us that we are all in need of forgiveness from God. We have all committed sin. *Ecclesiastes 7:20* proclaims, *"There is not a righteous man on earth who does what is right and never sins." 1 John 1:8* says, *"If we claim to be without sin, we deceive ourselves and the truth is not in us."* All sin is ultimately an act of rebellion against God *(Psalm 51:4)*. As a result, we desperately need God's forgiveness. If our sins are not forgiven, we will spend eternity suffering the consequences of our sins *(Matthew 25:46; John 3:36)*.
- **How do I get it?** Thankfully, God is loving and merciful; eager to forgive us of our sins! *2 Peter 3:9* tells us, *"...He is patient with you, not wanting anyone to perish, but everyone to come to repentance."* God desires to forgive us, so He provided for our forgiveness. The only just penalty for our sins is death. The first half of *Romans 6:23* declares, *"For the wages of sin is death..."* Eternal death is what we have earned for our sins. God, in His perfect plan, became a human being, Jesus Christ *(John 1:1, 14)*. Jesus died on the cross, taking the penalty that we deserve, death. *2 Corinthians 5:21* teaches us, *"God made Him who had no sin to be sin for us, so that in Him we might become the righteousness of God."* Jesus died on the cross, taking the punishment that we deserve! As God, Jesus' death provided forgiveness for the sins of the entire world. *1 John 2:2* proclaims, *"He is the atoning sacrifice for our sins, and not only for ours but also for the sins of the whole world."* Jesus rose from the dead, proclaiming His victory over sin and death *(1 Corinthians 15:1-28)*. Praise God, through the death and resurrection of Jesus Christ, the second half of *Romans 6:23* is true, *"...but the gift of God is eternal life through Jesus Christ our Lord."* Do you want to have your sins forgiven? Do you have a nagging feeling of guilt that you can't seem to get to go away? Forgiveness of your sins is available if you will place your faith in Jesus Christ as your Savior. *Ephesians 1:7* says, *"In Him we have redemption through His blood, the forgiveness of sins, in accordance with the riches of God's grace."* Jesus paid our debt for us, so we could be forgiven. All you have

to do is ask God to forgive you through Jesus, believing that Jesus died to pay for your forgiveness, and He will forgive you! *John 3:16-17* contains this wonderful message, *"For God so loved the world that He gave His one and only Son, that whoever believes in Him shall not perish but have eternal life. For God did not send His Son into the world to condemn the world, but to save the world through Him."*

- **Is it really that easy?** Yes it is that easy! You can't earn forgiveness from God. You can't pay for your forgiveness from God. You can only receive it, by faith, through the grace and mercy of God. If you want to accept Jesus Christ as your Savior and receive forgiveness from God, here is prayer you can pray. Saying this prayer or any other prayer will not save you. It is only trusting in Jesus Christ that can provide forgiveness of sins. This prayer is simply a way to express to God your faith in Him and thank Him for providing for your forgiveness. "God, I know that I have sinned against You and am deserving of punishment. But Jesus Christ took the punishment that I deserve so that through faith in Him I could be forgiven. I place my trust in You for salvation. Thank You for Your wonderful grace and forgiveness! Amen!"

Question: "What happens to those who have never heard about Jesus?"

All people are accountable to God whether they have "heard about Him" or not. The Bible tells us that God has clearly revealed Himself in nature *(Romans 1:20)* and in the hearts of people *(Ecclesiastes 3:11)*. The problem is that the human race is sinful; we all reject this knowledge of God and rebel against Him *(Romans 1:21-23)*. Apart from God's grace, God would give us over to the sinful desires of our hearts, allowing us to discover how useless and miserable life is apart from Him. This He does for those who reject Him *(Romans 1:24-32)*.

In reality, it is not that some people have not heard about God. Rather, the problem is that they have rejected what they have heard and what is readily seen in nature. *Deuteronomy 4:29* proclaims, *"But if from there you seek the LORD your God, you will find him if you look for him with all your heart and with all your soul."* This verse teaches an important principle: everyone who truly seeks after God will find Him. If a person truly desires to know God, God will make Himself known. The problem with this is, *"there is no one who understands, no one who seeks God" (Romans 3:11)*. People reject the knowledge of God that is present in nature and in their own heart, and instead decide to worship a "god" of their own creation. It is foolish to debate the fairness of God sending someone to hell who never had the opportunity to hear the Gospel of Christ. People are responsible to God for what God has already revealed to them. The Bible says that people reject this knowledge, and therefore God is just in condemning them to hell.

Instead of debating the fate of those who have never heard, we, as Christians, should be doing our best to make sure that they hear. We are called to spread the Gospel throughout the nations *(Matthew 28:19-20; Acts 1:8)*. The fact that we know people reject the knowledge of God revealed in nature must motivate us to proclaim the good news of salvation through Jesus Christ. Only through accepting the Gospel of God's grace through the Lord Jesus Christ can people be saved from their sins and rescued from an eternity apart from God in hell. If we assume that those who never hear the Gospel are granted mercy from God, we will run into a terrible problem. If people who never hear the Gospel are saved we should make sure that no one ever hears the Gospel. The worst thing we could do would be share the Gospel with a person and have him or her reject it. If that were to happen, he or she would be condemned. People who do not hear the Gospel must be condemned, or else there is no motive for evangelism. Why run the risk of people possibly rejecting the Gospel and condemning themselves – when they were previously saved because they had never heard the Gospel?

Question: "What happened to those who believed in God before Jesus?"

Since the fall of man, the basis of salvation has always been the death of Christ. No one, either prior to the cross or since the cross, would ever be saved without that one pivotal event in the history of the world.

Christ's death paid the penalty for past sins of Old Testament saints and future sins of New Testament saints.

The requirement for salvation has always been faith. The object of one's faith for salvation has always been God. The psalmist wrote, *"Blessed are all those who put their trust in Him" (Psalm 2:12). Genesis 15:6* tells us that Abraham believed God and that was enough for God to account it to him for righteousness, see also *Romans 4:3-8*. The Old Testament sacrificial system did not take away sin, as *Hebrews 9:1 -10:4* clearly teaches. It did, however, point to the day when the Son of God would shed His blood for the sinful human race.

What has changed through the ages is the content of a believer's faith. God's requirement of what must be believed is based on the amount of revelation He has given mankind up to that time. This is called progressive revelation. Adam believed the promise God gave in *Genesis 3:15* that the Seed of the woman would conquer Satan. Adam believed Him, demonstrated by the name he gave Eve *(v.20)* and the Lord indicated His acceptance immediately by covering them with coats of skin *(v.21)*. At that point that is all Adam knew, but he believed it.

Abraham believed God according to the promises and new revelation God gave him in *Genesis 12* and *15*. Prior to Moses, no Scripture was written, but mankind was responsible for what God had revealed. Throughout the Old Testament, believers came to salvation because they believed that God would someday take care of their sin problem. Today, we look back, believing that He has already taken care of our sins on Calvary *(John 3:16; Hebrews 9:28)*.

What about believers in Christ's day, prior to the cross and resurrection, what did they believe? Did they understand the full picture of Christ dying on a cross for their sins? Late in his ministry, *"Jesus began to show to His disciples that He must go to Jerusalem, and suffer many things from the elders and chief priests and scribes, and be killed, and be raised the third day" (Matthew 16:21)*. What was the reaction of His disciples to this message? *"Then Peter took Him aside and began to rebuke Him, saying, ''Far be it from you, Lord; this shall not happen to you!'" (16:22)*. Peter, and the other disciples, did not know the full truth, yet they were saved because they believed that God would take care of their sin problem. They didn't exactly know how He would accomplish that, any more than Adam, Abraham, Moses, or David knew how, but they believed God.

Today, we have more revelation than did people living before the resurrection of Christ, we know the full picture. *"God, who at various times and in various ways spoke in time past to the fathers by the prophets, has in these last days spoken to us by His Son" (Hebrews 1:1 -2)*. Our salvation is still based on the death of Christ, our faith is still the requirement for salvation, and the object of our faith is still God. Today for us the content of our faith is that Christ died for our sins, that He was buried, and that He rose the third day *(1 Corinthians 15:3-4)*.

Question: "Is salvation by faith alone, or by faith plus works?"

This is perhaps the most important question in all of Christian theology. This question is the cause of the Reformation - the split between the Protestant church and Catholic church. This question is a key difference between Biblical Christianity and most of the "Christian" cults. Is salvation by faith alone, or by faith plus works? Am I saved just by believing in Jesus, or do I have to believe in Jesus and do certain things?

The question of faith alone or faith plus works is made difficult by some hard-to-reconcile Bible passages. Compare *Romans 3:28, 5:1* and *Galatians 3:24* with *James 2:24*. Some see a difference between Paul (salvation is by faith alone) and James (salvation is by faith plus works). In reality, Paul and James did not disagree at all. The only point of disagreement some people claim is over the relationship between faith and works. Paul dogmatically says that justification is by faith alone *(Ephesians 2:8-9)* while James appears to be saying that justification is by faith plus works. This apparent problem is answered by examining what exactly James is talking about.

James is refuting the belief that a person can have faith without producing any good works *(James 2:17-18)*. James is emphasizing the point that genuine faith in Christ will produce a changed life and good works *(James 2:20-26)*. James is not saying that justification is by faith plus works, but rather that a person who is truly justified by faith will have good works in his life. If a person claims to be a believer, but has no good works in his life, then he likely does not have genuine faith in Christ *(James 2:14, 17, 20, 26)*.

Paul says the same thing in his writings. The good fruit believers should have in their lives is listed in *Galatians 5:22-23*. Immediately after telling us that we are saved by faith, not works in *Ephesians 2:8-9*, Paul informs us that we were created to do good works in *verse 10*. Paul expects just as much of a changed life as James does, *"Therefore, if anyone is in Christ, he is a new creation; the old has gone, the new has come" (2 Corinthians 5:17)!*

James and Paul do not disagree on their teaching on salvation. They approach the same subject from different perspectives. Paul simply emphasized that justification is by faith alone while James put emphasis on the fact that faith in Christ produces good works.

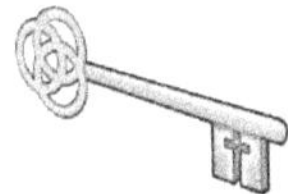

Question: "What is the Romans Road to salvation?"

The Romans Road to salvation is a way of explaining the good news of salvation using verses from the Book of Romans. It is a simple yet powerful method of explaining why we need salvation, how God provided salvation, how we can receive salvation, and what are the results of salvation.

The first verse on the Romans Road to salvation is *Romans 3:23, "For all have sinned, and come short of the glory of God."* We have all sinned. We have all done things that are displeasing to God. There is no one who is innocent. *Romans 3:10-18* gives a detailed picture of what sin looks like in our lives.

The second Scripture on the Romans Road to salvation, *Romans 6:23*, teaches us about the consequences of sin *"For the wages of sin is death; but the gift of God is eternal life through Jesus Christ our Lord."* The punishment that we have earned for our sins is death. Not just physical death, but eternal death!

The third verse on the Romans road to salvation picks up where *Romans 6:23* left off, *"but the gift of God is eternal life through Jesus Christ our Lord." Romans 5:8* declares, *"But God demonstrates His own love toward us, in that while we were still sinners, Christ died for us."* Jesus Christ died for us! Jesus' death paid for the price of our sins. Jesus' resurrection proves that God accepted Jesus' death as the payment for our sins.

The fourth stop on the Romans road to salvation is *Romans 10:9, "that if you confess with your mouth Jesus as Lord, and believe in your heart that God raised Him from the dead, you will be saved."* Because of Jesus' death on our behalf all we have to do is believe in Him, trusting His death as the payment for our sins, and we will be saved! *Romans 10:13* says it again, *"for everyone who calls on the name of the Lord will be saved."* Jesus died to pay the penalty for our sins and rescue us from eternal death. Salvation, the forgiveness of sins, is available to anyone who will trust in Jesus Christ as their Lord and Savior.

The final aspect of the Romans Road to salvation is the results of salvation. *Romans 5:1* has this wonderful message, *"Therefore, since we have been justified through faith, we have peace with God through our Lord Jesus Christ."* Through Jesus Christ we can have a relationship of peace with God. *Romans 8:1* teaches us, *"Therefore, there is now no condemnation for those who are in Christ Jesus."* Because of Jesus' death on our behalf, we will never be condemned for our sins. Finally, we have this precious promise of God from *Romans 8:38-39*, *"For I am convinced that neither death nor life, neither angels nor demons, neither the present nor the future, nor any powers, neither height nor depth, nor anything else in all creation, will be able to separate us from the love of God that is in Christ Jesus our Lord."*

Would you like to follow the Romans Road to salvation? If so, here is a simple prayer you can pray to God. Saying this prayer is a way to declare to God that you are relying on Jesus Christ for your salvation. The words themselves will not save you. Only faith in Jesus Christ can provide salvation! "God, I know that I have sinned against you and am deserving of punishment. But Jesus Christ took the punishment that I deserve so that through faith in Him I could be forgiven. With your help, I place my trust in You for salvation. Thank You for Your wonderful grace and forgiveness - the gift of eternal life! Amen!"

Question: "How can I have assurance of my salvation?"

How can you know for sure if you are saved? Consider *1 John 5:11-13 (NLT)*: *"And this is what God has testified: He has given us eternal life, and this life is in his Son. So whoever has God's Son has life; whoever does not have his Son does not have life. I write this to you who believe in the Son of God, so that you may know you have eternal life."* Who is it that has the Son? Those who have believed in Him and accepted Him *(John 1:12)*. If you have Jesus you have life, Eternal life.

God wants us to have assurance of our salvation. We cannot live our Christian lives wondering and worrying each day whether we are truly saved or not. That is why the Bible makes the plan of salvation so clear. Believe in Jesus Christ and you will be saved *(John 3:16; Acts 16:31)*. Do you believe that Jesus is the Savior, that He died to pay the penalty for your sins *(Romans 5:8; 2 Corinthians 5:21)*? Are you trusting in Him alone for salvation? If your answer is yes, you are saved! Assurance means to *"put beyond all doubt."* By taking God's Word to heart, you can *"put beyond all doubt"* the fact and reality of your eternal salvation.

Jesus Himself states this regarding those who have believed in Him: *"I give them eternal life, and they will never perish. No one will snatch them away from me, for my Father has given them to me, and he is more powerful than anyone else. So no one can take them from me" (John 10:28-29 NLT)*. Again, this gives more emphasis to "eternal." Eternal life is just that, eternal. There is nobody, not even yourself, who can take Christ's God-given gift of salvation away from you.

Memorize these passages. We hide God's Word in our hearts so that we do not sin against Him *(Psalm 119:11)*, and this includes doubt. Take joy in what God's Word is saying to you: That instead of doubt we can live with confidence! We can have the assurance from Christ's own Word that the state of our salvation will never be in question. Our assurance is based on God's love for us through Jesus Christ. *Jude 24-25, "To Him who is able to keep you from falling and to present you before his glorious presence without fault and with great joy - to the only God our Savior be glory, majesty, power and authority, through Jesus Christ our Lord, before all ages, now and forevermore! Amen."*

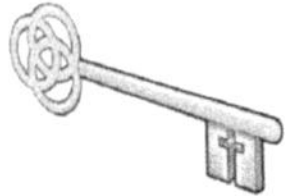

Question: "Is baptism necessary for salvation? What is baptismal regeneration?"

Baptismal regeneration is the belief that a person must be baptized in order to be saved. It is our contention that baptism is an important step of obedience for a Christian, but we adamantly reject baptism as being required for salvation. We strongly believe that each and every Christian should be water baptized by immersion. Baptism illustrates a believer's identification with Christ's death, burial, and resurrection. *Romans 6:3-4* declares, *"Or don't you know that all of us who were baptized into Christ Jesus were baptized into His death? We were therefore buried with Him through baptism into death in order that, just as Christ was raised from the dead through the glory of the Father, we too may live a new life."* The action of being immersed in the water illustrates being buried with Christ. The action of coming out of the water pictures Christ's resurrection.

Anything in addition to faith in Jesus Christ as being required for salvation is a works-based salvation. To add ANYTHING to the Gospel is to say that Jesus' death on the cross was not sufficient to purchase our salvation. To say that we must be baptized in order to be saved is to say that we must add our own good works and obedience to Christ's death in order to make it sufficient for salvation. Jesus' death alone paid for our sins *(Romans 5:8; 2 Corinthians 5:21)*. Jesus' payment for our sins is appropriated to our "account" by faith alone *(John 3:16; Acts 16:31; Ephesians 2:8-9)*. Therefore, baptism is an important step of obedience after salvation, but cannot be a requirement for salvation.

Yes, there are some verses that seem to indicate baptism as a necessary requirement for salvation. However, since the Bible so clearly tells us that salvation is received by faith alone *(John 3:16; Ephesians 2:8-9; Titus 3:5)*, there must be a different interpretation of those verses. Scripture does not contradict Scripture. In Bible times, a person who converted from one religion to another was often baptized to identify conversion. Baptism was the means of making a decision public. Those who refused to be baptized were saying they did not truly believe. So, in the minds of the apostles and early disciples, the idea of an unbaptized believer was unheard of. When a person claimed to believe in Christ, yet was ashamed to proclaim his faith in public, it indicated that he did not have true faith.

If baptism is necessary for salvation, why would Paul have said, *"I am thankful that I did not baptize any of you except Crispus and Gaius" (1 Corinthians 1:14)*? Why would he have said, *"For Christ did not send me to baptize, but to preach the gospel - not with words of human wisdom, lest the cross of Christ be emptied of its power" (1 Corinthians 1:17)*? Granted, in this passage Paul is arguing against the divisions that plagued the Corinthian church. However, how could Paul possibly say, *"I am thankful that I did not baptize..."* or *"For Christ did not send me to baptize..."* if baptism were necessary for salvation? If baptism is necessary for salvation, Paul would literally be saying, *"I am thankful that you were not saved..."* and *"For Christ did not send me to save..."* That would be an unbelievably ridiculous statement for Paul to make. Further, when Paul gives a detailed outline of what he considers the Gospel *(1 Corinthians 15:1-8)*, why does he neglect to mention baptism? If baptism is a requirement for salvation, how could any presentation of the Gospel lack a mentioning of baptism?

Baptismal regeneration is not a Biblical concept. Baptism does not save from sin, but from a bad conscience. Peter clearly taught that baptism was not a ceremonial act of physical purification, but the pledge of a good conscience toward God. Baptism is the symbol of what has already occurred in the heart and life of one who has trusted Christ as Savior *(Romans 6:3-5; Galatians 3:27; Colossians 2:12)*. To make the source of salvation perfectly clear, Peter added, *"by the resurrection of Jesus Christ" (1 Peter 1:3)*. Baptism is an important step of obedience that every Christian should take. Baptism cannot be a requirement for salvation. To make it such is an attack on the sufficiency of the death and resurrection of Jesus Christ.

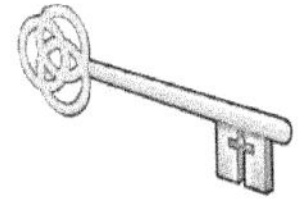

Question: "Does *Acts 2:38* teach that baptism is necessary for salvation?"

Acts 2:38, "And Peter said to them, 'Repent, and let each of you be baptized in the name of Jesus Christ for the forgiveness of your sins; and you shall receive the gift of the Holy Spirit.'" As with any single verse or passage, we discern what it teaches by first filtering it through what we know the Bible teaches on the subject at hand. In the case of baptism and salvation, the Bible is clear that salvation is by grace through faith in Jesus Christ, not by works of any kind, including baptism *(Ephesians 2:8-9)*. So, any interpretation which comes to the conclusion that baptism, or any other act, is necessary for salvation, is a faulty interpretation.

Why, then, do some come to the conclusion that we must be baptized in order to be saved? Often, the discussion of whether or not this passage teaches baptism is required for salvation centers around the Greek word eis that is translated "for" in this passage. Those who hold to the belief that baptism is required for salvation are quick to point to this verse and the fact that it says "be baptized in the name of Jesus Christ for the forgiveness of your sins," assuming that the word translated "for" in this verse means "in order to get." However, in both Greek and English, there are many possible usages of the word "for."

As an example, when one says "Take two aspirin for your headache," it is obvious to everybody that it does not mean "take two aspirin in order to get your headache," but instead to "take two aspirin because you already have a headache." There are three possible meanings of the word "for" that might fit the context of *Acts 2:38*:

1. "in order to be, become, get, have, keep, etc.,"
2. "because of, as the result of," or
3. "with regard to."

Since any one of the three meanings could fit the context of this passage, additional study is required in order to determine which one is correct.

We need to start by looking back to the original language and the meaning of the Greek word "eis". This is a common Greek word that is translated many different ways; it is used 1774 times in the New Testament. Like the English word "for" it can have several different meanings. So, again, we see at least two or three possible meanings of the passage, one that would seem to support that baptism is required for salvation and others that would not. While both the meanings of the Greek word eis are seen in different passages of Scripture, such noted Greek scholars as A.T. Robertson and J.R. Mantey have maintained that the Greek preposition eis in *Acts 2:38* should be translated "because of" or "in view of," and not "in order to," or "for the purpose of."

One example of how this preposition is used in other Scriptures is seen in *Matthew 12:41* where the word eis communicates the "result" of an action. In this case it is said that the people of Nineveh *"repented at the preaching of Jonah"*, the word translated "at" is the same Greek word eis. Clearly, the meaning of this passage is that they repented "because of"" or "as the result of" Jonah's preaching. In the same way, it would be possible that *Acts 2:38* is indeed communicating the fact that they were to be baptized "as the result of" or "because" they already had believed and in doing so had already received forgiveness of their sins *(John 1:12; John 3:14-18; John 5:24; John 11:25-26; Acts 10:43; Acts 13:39; Acts 16:31; Acts 26:18; Romans 10:9; Ephesians 1:12-14)*. This interpretation of the passage is also consistent with the message recorded in Peter's next two sermons to unbelievers where he associates the forgiveness of sins with the act of repentance and faith in Christ without even mentioning baptism *(Acts 3:17-26; Acts 4:8-12)*.

In addition to *Acts 2:38*, there are three other verses where the Greek word eis is used in conjunction with the word "baptize" or "baptism." The first of these is *Matthew 3:11*, *"baptize you with water for repentance."* Clearly the Greek word eis cannot mean "in order to get" in this passage. They were not baptized "in order to get repentance," but were "baptized because they had repented." The second passage is *Romans 6:3* where we have the phrase *"baptized into (eis) His death."* This again fits with the meaning "because of" or in "regard to." The third and final passage is *1 Corinthians 10:2* and the phrase *"baptized into (eis) Moses in the cloud and in the sea."* Again, eis cannot mean "in order to get" in this passage because the Israelites were not baptized in order to get Moses to be their leader, but because he was their leader and had led them out of Egypt. If one is consistent with the way the preposition eis is used in conjunction with baptism, we must conclude that *Acts 2:38* is indeed referring to their being baptized "because" they had received forgiveness of their sins. Some other verses where the Greek preposition eis does not mean "in order to obtain" are *Matthew 28:19; 1 Peter 3:21; Acts 19:3; 1 Corinthians 1:15; and 12:13.*

The grammatical evidence surrounding this verse and the preposition eis are clear that while both views on this verse are well within the context and the range of possible meanings of the passage, the majority of the evidence is in favor that the best possible definition of the word "for" in this context is either "because of" or "in regard to" and not "in order to get." Therefore, *Acts 2:38*, when interpreted correctly, does not teach that baptism is required for salvation.

Besides the precise meaning of the preposition translated "for" in this passage, there is another grammatical aspect of this verse to carefully consider; the change between the second person and third person between the verbs and pronouns in the passage. For example, in Peter's commands to repent and be baptized the Greek verb translated "repent" is in the second person plural while the verb "be baptized," is in the third person singular. When we couple this with the fact that the pronoun "your" in the phrase "forgiveness of your sins" is also second person plural, we see an important distinction being made that helps us understand this passage. The result of this change from second person plural to third person singular and back would seem to connect the phrase "forgiveness of your sins" directly with the command to "repent." Therefore, when you take into account the change in person and plurality, essentially what you have is "You (plural) repent for the forgiveness of your (plural) sins, and let each one (singular) of you be baptized (singular)." Or, to put it in a more distinct way: "You all repent for the forgiveness of all of your sins, and let each one of you be baptized."

Another error that is made by those who believe *Acts 2:38* teaches baptism is required for salvation is what is sometimes called the Negative Inference Fallacy. Simply put, this is the idea that just because a statement is true, we cannot assume all negations (or opposites) of that statement are true. In other words, just because *Acts 2:38* says *"repent and be baptized....for the forgiveness of sins...and the gift of the Holy Spirit,"* it does not mean that if one repents and is not baptized, he will not receive forgiveness of sins or the gift of the Holy Spirit.

There is an important difference between a condition of salvation and a requirement for salvation. The Bible is clear that belief is both a condition and a requirement, but the same cannot be said for baptism. The

Bible does not say that if a man is not baptized then he will not be saved. If that were true, Jesus would never have been able to assure the criminal crucified with Him that he would be with Him in paradise that very day *(Luke 23:39-43)*. One can add any number of conditions to faith, which is required for salvation, and the person can still be saved. For example if a person believes, is baptized, goes to church, and gives to the poor he will be saved. Where the error in thinking occurs is if one assumes all these other conditions, "baptism, going to church, giving to the poor," are required for one to be saved. While they might be the evidence of salvation, they are not a requirement for salvation.

The fact that baptism is not required to receive forgiveness and the gift of the Holy Spirit should also be evident by simply reading a little farther in the *Book of Acts*. In *Acts 10:43*, Peter tells Cornelius that *"through His name everyone who believes in Him receives forgiveness of sins."* Please note that nothing at this point has been mentioned about being baptized, yet Peter connects believing in Christ with the act of receiving forgiveness for sins. The next thing that happens is, having believed Peter's message about Christ, the *"Holy Spirit fell upon all those who were listening to the message" (Acts 10:44)*. It is only after they had believed, and therefore received forgiveness of their sins and the gift of the Holy Spirit, that Cornelius and his household were baptized *(Acts 10:47-48)*. The context and the passage are very clear; Cornelius and his household received both forgiveness of sins and the Holy Spirit before they were ever baptized. In fact, the reason Peter allowed them to be baptized was that they showed evidence of receiving the Holy Spirit *"just as Peter and the Jewish believers"* had.

In conclusion, *Acts 2:38* does not teach that baptism is required for salvation. While baptism is important as the sign that one has been justified by faith and as the public declaration of one's faith in Christ and membership in a local body of believers, it is not the means of remission or forgiveness of sins. The Bible is very clear that we are saved by grace alone through faith alone in Christ alone *(John 1:12; John 3:16; Acts 16:31; Romans 3:21-30; Romans 4:5; Romans 10:9-10; Ephesians 2:8-10; Philippians 3:9; Galatians 2:16)*.

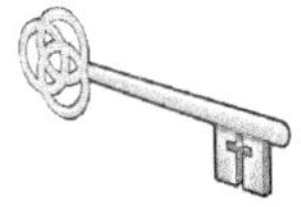

Question: "Does *Mark 16:16* teach that baptism is necessary for salvation?"

As with any single verse or passage, we discern what it teaches by first filtering it through what we know the Bible teaches on the subject at hand. In the case of baptism and salvation, the Bible is clear that salvation is by grace through faith in Jesus Christ, not by works of any kind, including baptism (*Ephesians 2:8 & 9*). So, any interpretation which comes to the conclusion that baptism, or any other act, is necessary for salvation, is a faulty interpretation.

In regard to *Mark 16:16*, it is important to remember that there are some textual issues with *Mark 16:9-20*. There is some question as to whether these verses were originally part of the Gospel of Mark, or whether they were added later by a scribe. As a result, it is best not to base a key doctrine on anything from *Mark 16:9-20*, such as snake-handling, unless it is also supported by other Scriptures.

Assuming that *verse 16* was included in Mark's original manuscript, does it teach that baptism is required for salvation? The simple answer is: No, it does not. In fact, when one carefully examines this verse, it becomes clear that in order to make this it teach that baptism is required for salvation, one must go beyond what the verse actually says. What this verse does teach is that belief is necessary for salvation, which is consistent with all other verses in the Bible that deal with salvation, especially the countless verses where only belief or faith is mentioned (e.g. *John 3:18; John 5:24; John 12:44; John 20:31; 1 John 5:13*).

"He who believes and is baptized will be saved; but he who does not believe will be condemned" (*Mark 16:16*). If we look at this verse closely, we see that it is composed of two basic statements. 1—He who believes and is baptized will be saved. 2—He who does not believe will be condemned.

Clearly, the determining factor regarding whether one is saved or condemned is whether or not he believes. In interpreting this passage correctly, it is important to realize that while it tells us something about believers who have been baptized (they are saved), it does not say anything about believers who have not been baptized. In order for this verse to teach that baptism is necessary for salvation, a third statement would have had to be included, that statement being: "He who believes and is not baptized will be condemned" or "He who is not baptized will be condemned." But, of course, neither of these statements is found in the verse.

Those who try to use *Mark 16:16* to teach that baptism is necessary for salvation commit a common but serious logical fallacy that is sometimes called the Negative Inference Fallacy. This fallacy can be stated as follows: "If a statement is true, we cannot assume that all negations (or opposites) of that statement are also true." In other words, just because *Mark 16:16* says that *"he who believes and is baptized will be saved"* it does not mean that if one believes, but is not baptized, he will not be saved. Yet, this is exactly what is assumed by those that look to this verse to support the view that baptism is necessary for salvation.

Often when considering logical fallacies, it can be helpful to look at other examples of the same fallacy. This will help us see the fallacy that is being committed more clearly. In this case let's consider two different but similarly structured statements. The first one is made considering the devastating hurricane that destroyed much of New Orleans in the fall of 2005. As a result of that hurricane, many lives were lost, and whole areas of New Orleans were destroyed. With that scenario in mind let's consider the first statement that is very similar in structure to what we find in *Mark 16:16*. "Those who left their homes and fled from New Orleans were saved; those who stayed in their homes perished."

Now, if we use the same logic on this statement as those that believe that *Mark 16:16* teaches that baptism is necessary for salvation, then we would have to conclude that if both the first conditions were not met (1—leaving their homes, 2—fleeing from New Orleans,) then everyone else would perish. Yet, in real life we know this was not true. Some people did stay in their homes in the low-lying areas and did not perish. In this situation it is easy to see that while the first statement is true, it is not true to assume that all those that did not flee New Orleans perished. Yet, if we use the same logic being used by those that say that *Mark 16:16* teaches that baptism is necessary for salvation, that is the conclusion that must be reached. Yet, it is clearly an erroneous conclusion.

Another example we might consider would be this statement: "Whoever believes and lives in Kansas will be saved, those that do not believe are condemned." Again take note of the similar structure as is found in *Mark 16:16*, and yet once again, it becomes clear that to say that only believers who live in Kansas are saved is an illogical and false assumption. While *Mark 16:16* does tell us something about believers who have been baptized (they will be saved), again, it says nothing about believers who have not been baptized.

"Whoever believes and lives in Kansas will be saved." *"Whoever believes and is baptized will be saved" (Mark 16:16)*. While both of these statements are true, we should notice that the first statement says nothing about people who believe and don't live in Kansas. And in the same way, *Mark 16:16* tells us nothing about believers who have not been baptized. It is a logical fallacy and false assumption, to make the first statement say that you have to live in Kansas to be saved, or the second statement say that you have to be baptized to be saved.

It is important to realize that just because *Mark 16:16* has two conditions relating to salvation (believe and be baptized), it does not mean that both conditions are requirements for being saved. This would also hold true if a third condition was added. Whether it is two or three conditions in a statement about salvation, the fact is, that does not mean that all three conditions must be met for one to be saved. In fact, we can add any number of secondary conditions to belief, such as if you believe and are baptized you will be saved, or if you believe, are baptized, go to church, and tithe you will be saved. However, to imply that all these conditions are requirements for salvation is incorrect.

This is important to realize because in order to know that a specific condition is required for salvation, we must have a negation statement as we have in the second part of *Mark 16:16: "whoever does not believe will be condemned."* In essence what Jesus has done in this verse is give us both the positive condition of belief (whoever believes will be saved) and the negative condition of unbelief (whoever does not believe will be condemned.) Therefore, we can say with absolute certainty that belief is a requirement for salvation. Even more importantly, we see both these positive and negative conditions over and over in Scripture (*John 3:16; John 3:18; John 3:36; John 5:24; John 6:53-54; John 8:24; Acts 16:31*).

While Jesus does give the positive condition of baptism (whoever is baptized) in *Mark 16:16* and other verses, nowhere in the Bible do we find the negative condition of baptism being taught (such as whoever is not baptized will be condemned). Therefore, we cannot say that baptism is necessary for salvation based on *Mark 16:16* (or any other similar verse). Those that do so are basing their argument on faulty logic.

Does *Mark 16:16* teach that baptism is or is not necessary for salvation? No it does not. It very clearly establishes that belief is a requirement for salvation, but does not prove or disprove whether baptism is a condition or requirement for salvation. How can we know, then, if one must be baptized in order to be saved? We must look to the full counsel of God's word to establish this. To summarize the evidence against baptism being required for salvation:

1) The Bible is clear that we are saved by faith alone. Abraham was saved by faith, and we are saved by faith (*Romans 4:1-25; Galatians 3:6-22*).
2) Throughout the Bible, in every dispensation, people have been saved without being baptized. Every believer in the Old Testament (e.g. Abraham, Jacob, David, Solomon) was saved but not baptized. The thief on the cross was saved but not baptized. Cornelius was saved before he was baptized (*Acts 10:44-46*).
3) Baptism is a testimony of our faith and a public declaration that we believe in Jesus Christ. The Scriptures clearly tell us that we have eternal life the moment we believe (*John 5:24*), and belief always comes before being baptized. Baptism does not save us any more than walking an aisle or saying a prayer saves us. We are saved when we believe.
4) The Bible never says that if one is not baptized then he is not saved.
5) If baptism is required for salvation, it means no one can be saved without a third party being present. In other words, if baptism is required for salvation, someone must baptize a person before he can be saved. This effectively limits who can be saved and when he can be saved. It means that someone who believes in and trusts in the death, burial, and resurrection of Jesus Christ, but does not have the chance of being baptized, cannot be saved. The consequences of this doctrine, when carried to its logical conclusion, are devastating. A soldier who believes but is killed in battle before he can be baptized would perish, etc.
6) Throughout the Bible we see that at the point of faith or belief, a believer possesses all the promises and blessings of salvation (*John 1:12; 3:16; 5:24; 6:47; 20:31; Acts 10:43; 13:39; 16:31*). When one believes, he has eternal life, does not come under judgment, and has passed from death into life (*John 5:24*), all before he/she is baptized.

If someone believes in baptismal regeneration, he/she would do well to prayerfully and carefully consider who or what they are really putting their faith and trust in. Is faith being placed in an act (being baptized) or on the finished work of Christ on the cross? Whom or what is being trusted for salvation? Could it be that it is the shadow (baptism) instead of the substance (Jesus Christ)? We must never forget that our faith must rest in Christ alone because "we have redemption through His blood, the forgiveness of our trespasses, according to the riches of His grace" (*Ephesians 1:7*).

Question: "Does *1 Peter 3:21* teach that baptism is necessary for salvation?"

As with any single verse or passage, we discern what it teaches by first filtering it through what we know the Bible teaches on the subject at hand. In the case of baptism and salvation, the Bible is clear that salvation is by grace through faith in Jesus Christ, not by works of any kind, including baptism (*Ephesians 2:8-9*). So, any interpretation which comes to the conclusion that baptism, or any other act, is necessary for salvation, is a faulty interpretation.

Those who believe that baptism is required for salvation are quick to use *1 Peter 3:21* as a "proof text," because it states "baptism now saves you." Was Peter really saying that the act of being baptized is what saves us? If he were, he would be contradicting many other passages of Scripture that clearly show people being saved (as evidenced by their receiving the Holy Spirit) prior to being baptized or without being baptized at all (like the thief on the cross in *Luke 23:39-43*). A good example of someone who was saved before being baptized is Cornelius and his household in *Acts 10*. We know that they were saved before being baptized because they had received the Holy Spirit, which is the evidence of salvation (*Romans 8:9; Ephesians 1:13; 1 John 3:24*). The evidence of their salvation was the reason Peter allowed them to be baptized. Countless passages of Scripture clearly teach that salvation comes when one believes in the gospel, at which time he or she is sealed *"in Christ with the Holy Spirit of promise"* (*Ephesians 1:13*).

Thankfully, though, we don't have to guess at what Peter means in this verse because he clarifies that for us with the phrase *"not the removal of dirt from the flesh, but an appeal to God for a good conscience."* While Peter is connecting baptism with salvation, it is not the act of being baptized that he is referring to (not the removal of dirt from the flesh). Being immersed in water does nothing but wash away dirt. What Peter is referring to is what baptism represents, which is what saves us (an appeal to God for a good conscience through the resurrection of Jesus Christ). In other words, Peter is simply connecting baptism with belief. It is not the getting-wet part that saves but is the *"appeal to God for a clean conscience"* which is signified by baptism, that saves us. The appeal to God always comes first. First belief and repentance, then we are baptized to publicly identify ourselves with Christ.

An excellent explanation of this passage is given by Dr. Kenneth Wuest, author of Word Studies in the Greek New Testament:

> *"Water baptism is clearly in the apostle's mind, not the baptism by the Holy Spirit, for he speaks of the waters of the flood as saving the inmates of the ark, and in this verse, of baptism saving believers. But he says that it saves them only as a counterpart. That is, water baptism is the counterpart of the reality, salvation. It can only save as a counterpart, not actually. The Old Testament sacrifices were counterparts of the reality, the Lord Jesus. They did not actually save the believer, only in type. It is not argued here that these sacrifices are analogous to Christian water baptism. The author is merely using them as an illustration of the use of the word 'counterpart.'*
>
> *So water baptism only saves the believer in type. The Old Testament Jew was saved before he brought the offering. That offering was only his outward testimony that he was placing faith in the Lamb of God of whom these sacrifices were a type......Water baptism is the outward testimony of the believer's inward faith. The person is saved the moment he places his faith in the Lord Jesus. Water baptism is the visible testimony to his faith and the salvation he was given in answer to that faith. Peter is careful to inform his readers that he is not teaching baptismal regeneration, namely, that a person who submits to baptism is thereby regenerated, for he says, 'not the putting away of the filth of the flesh.' Baptism, Peter explains, does not wash away the filth of the flesh, either in a literal sense as a bath for the body, nor in a metaphorical sense as a cleansing for the soul. No ceremonies really affect the conscience. But he defines what he means by salvation, in the words 'the answer of a good conscience toward*

God' and he explains how this is accomplished, namely, 'by the resurrection of Jesus Christ' in that the believing sinner is identified with Him in that resurrection."

Part of the confusion on this passage comes from the fact that in many ways the purpose of baptism as a public declaration of one's faith in Christ and identification with Him has been replaced by "making a decision for Christ" or "praying a sinner's prayer." Baptism has been relegated to something that is done later. Yet to Peter or any of the first -century Christians, the idea that a person would confess Christ as his Savior and not be baptized as soon as possible would have been unheard of. Therefore, it is not surprising that Peter would see baptism as almost synonymous with salvation. Yet Peter makes it clear in this verse that it is not the ritual itself that saves, but the fact that we are united with Christ in His resurrection through faith, *"the pledge of a good conscience toward God through the resurrection of Jesus Christ"* (*1 Peter 3:21*).

Therefore, the baptism that Peter says saves us is the one that is preceded by faith in the propitiatory sacrifice of Christ that justifies the unrighteous sinner (*Romans 3:25-26; 4:5*). Baptism is the outward sign of what God has done *"by the washing of regeneration and renewing by the Holy Spirit"* (*Titus 3:5*).

Question: "Does *John 3:5* teach that baptism is necessary for salvation?"

As with any single verse or passage, we discern what it teaches by first filtering it through what we know the Bible teaches on the subject at hand. In the case of baptism and salvation, the Bible is clear that salvation is by grace through faith in Jesus Christ, not by works of any kind, including baptism (*Ephesians 2:8-9*). So, any interpretation which comes to the conclusion that baptism, or any other act, is necessary for salvation, is a faulty interpretation.

John 3:3-7, "Jesus answered and said to him, 'Truly, truly, I say to you, unless one is born again, he cannot see the kingdom of God.'

Nicodemus said to Him, 'How can a man be born when he is old? He cannot enter a second time into his mother's womb and be born, can he?' Jesus answered, 'Truly, truly, I say to you, unless one is born of water and the Spirit, he cannot enter into the kingdom of God. That which is born of the flesh is flesh, and that which is born of the Spirit is spirit. Do not marvel that I said to you, 'You must be born again.'"

When first considering this passage, it is important to note that nowhere in the context of the passage is baptism even mentioned. While baptism is mentioned later in this chapter (*John 3:22-30*), that is in a totally different setting (Judea instead of Jerusalem) and at a different time from the discussion with Nicodemus. This is not to say Nicodemus was unfamiliar with baptism, either from the Jewish practice of baptizing Gentile converts to Judaism, or from John the Baptist's ministry. However, simply reading these verses in context would give one no reason to assume Jesus was speaking of baptism, unless one was looking to read into the passage a preconceived idea or theology. To automatically read baptism into this verse simply because it mentions "water" is unwarranted.

Those who hold baptism to be required for salvation point to "born of water" as evidence. As one person has put it, "Jesus describes it and tells him plainly how—by being born of water and the Spirit. This is a perfect description of baptism! Jesus could not have given a more detailed and accurate explanation of baptism." However, had Jesus actually wanted to say that one must be baptized to be saved, He clearly could have simply stated, "Truly, truly, I say to you, unless one is baptized and born of the Spirit, he cannot enter into the kingdom of God." Further, if Jesus had made such a statement, He would have contradicted numerous other Bible passages that make it clear that salvation is by faith (*John 3:16; John 3:36; Ephesians 2:8-9: Titus 3:5*).

We should also not lose sight of the fact that when Jesus was speaking to Nicodemus, the ordinance of Christian baptism was not yet in effect. This important inconsistency in interpreting Scripture is seen when one asks those who believe baptism is required for salvation why the thief on the cross did not need to be baptized to be saved. A common reply to that question is: "The thief on the cross was still under the Old Covenant and therefore not subject to this baptism. He was saved just like anyone else under the Old Covenant." So, in essence, the same people who say the thief did not need to be baptized because he was "under the Old Covenant" will use *John 3:5* as "proof" that baptism is necessary for salvation. They insist that Jesus is telling Nicodemus that he must be baptized to be saved, even though he too was under the Old Covenant. If the thief on the cross was saved without being baptized (because he was under the Old Covenant), why would Jesus tell Nicodemus (who was also under the Old Covenant) that he needed to be baptized?

If "being born of water and the Spirit" is not referring to baptism, then what does it mean? Traditionally, there have been two interpretations of this phrase. The first is that being "born of water" is being used by Jesus to refer to natural birth (with water referring to the amniotic fluid that surrounds the baby in the womb) and that being born of the "Spirit" indicates spiritual birth. While that is certainly a possible interpretation of the term "born of water" and would seem to fit the context of Nicodemus' question about how a man could be born "when he is old," it is not the best interpretation given the context of this passage. After all, Jesus was not talking about the difference between natural birth and spiritual birth. What He was doing was explaining to Nicodemus his need to be "born from above" or "born again."

The second common interpretation of this passage and the one that best fits the overall context, not only of this passage but of the Bible as a whole, is the one that sees the phrase "born of water and the Spirit" as both describing different aspects of the same spiritual birth, or of what it means to be "born again" or "born from above." So, when Jesus told Nicodemus that he must "be born of water and the Spirit," He was not referring to literal water (i.e. baptism or the amniotic fluid in the womb), but was referring to the need for spiritual cleansing or renewal. Throughout the Old Testament (*Psalm 51:2,7; Ezekiel 36:25*) and the New Testament (*John 13:10; 15:3; 1 Corinthians 6:11; Hebrews 10:22*), water is often used figuratively of spiritual cleansing or regeneration that is brought forth by the Holy Spirit, through the Word of God, at the moment of salvation (*Ephesians 5:26; Titus 3:5*).

The Barclay Daily Study Bible describes this concept in this way:

> *"There are two thoughts here. Water is the symbol of cleansing. When Jesus takes possession of our lives, when we love Him with all our heart, the sins of the past are forgiven and forgotten. The Spirit is the symbol of power. When Jesus takes possession of our lives it is not only that the past is forgotten and forgiven; if that were all, we might well proceed to make the same mess of life all*

over again; but into life there enters a new power which enables us to be what by ourselves we could never be and to do what by ourselves we could never do. Water and the Spirit stand for the cleansing and the strengthening power of Christ, which wipes out the past and gives victory in the future."

Therefore, the water mentioned in this verse is not literal physical water but rather the *"living water"* Jesus promised the woman at the well in *John 4:10* and the people in Jerusalem in *John 7:37-39*. It is the inward purification and renewal produced by the Holy Spirit that brings forth spiritual life to a dead sinner (*Ezekiel 36:25-27; Titus 3:5*). Jesus reinforces this truth in *John 3:7* when He restates that one must be born again and that this newness of life can only be produced by the Holy Spirit (*John 3:8*).

There are several reasons why this is the correct interpretation of the phrase "born of water and the Spirit":

1) We should note that the Greek word translated "again" has two possible meanings. The first one is "again," and the second one is "from above." Nicodemus apparently assumed the first meaning "again" and found that idea incomprehensible. That is why he could not understand how as a grown man he could re-enter his mother's womb and be "born again" physically. Therefore, Jesus restates what He had just told Nicodemus in a different way so that it would be clear He was referring to being "born from above." In other words, both "born from above" and "born of water and Spirit" are two ways of saying the same thing.
2) It is important to note the Greek grammar in this verse would seem to indicate "being born of water" and "being born of the Spirit" are thought of as one item, not two. Therefore, it is not speaking of two separate births, as Nicodemus incorrectly thought, but of one birth, that of being "born from above" or the spiritual birth that is necessary for anyone to "see the kingdom of God." This need for one to be "born again," or to experience spiritual birth, is so important that Jesus tells Nicodemus of its necessity three different times in this passage of Scripture (*John 3:3, 3:5, 3:7*).
3) Water is often used symbolically in the Bible to refer to the work of the Holy Spirit in sanctifying a believer, whereby God cleanses and purifies the believer's heart or soul. In many places in both the Old and New Testaments, the work of the Holy Spirit is compared to water (*Isaiah 44:3; John 7:38-39*).

Jesus rebukes Nicodemus in *John 3:10* by asking him: *"Are you the teacher of Israel, and do not understand these things?"* This implies that what Jesus had just told him was something Nicodemus should have known and understood from the Old Testament. What is it that Nicodemus, as a teacher of the Old Testament, should have known and understood? It is that God had promised in the Old Testament a time was coming in which He would: *"sprinkle clean water on you, and you will be clean; I will cleanse you from all your filthiness and from all your idols. Moreover, I will give you a new heart and put a new spirit within you; and I will remove the heart of stone from your flesh and give you a heart of flesh. I will put My Spirit within you and cause you to walk in My statutes, and you will be careful to observe My ordinances."* (*Ezekiel 36:25-27*). Jesus rebuked Nicodemus because he failed to recall and understand one of the key Old Testament passages pertaining to the New Covenant (*Jeremiah 31:33*). Nicodemus should have been expecting this. Why would Jesus have rebuked Nicodemus for not understanding baptism considering the fact that baptism is nowhere mentioned in the Old Testament?

While this verse does not teach baptism is required for salvation, we should be careful not to neglect baptism's importance. Baptism is the sign or the symbol for what takes place when one is born again. Baptism's importance should not be downplayed or minimized. However, baptism does not save us. What saves us is the cleansing work of the Holy Spirit, when we are born again and regenerated by the Holy Spirit (*Titus 3:5*).

Question: "Does *Acts 22:16* teach that baptism is necessary for salvation?"

As with any single verse or passage, we discern what it teaches by first filtering it through what we know the Bible teaches on the subject at hand. In the case of baptism and salvation, the Bible is clear that salvation is by grace through faith in Jesus Christ, not by works of any kind, including baptism (*Ephesians 2:8-9*). So, any interpretation which comes to the conclusion that baptism, or any other act, is necessary for salvation, is a faulty interpretation.

Acts 22:16, "And now what are you waiting for? Get up, be baptized and wash your sins away, calling on his name." The first question that must be answered is "when was Paul saved?" *1. Paul* tells that he did not receive or hear the Gospel from Ananias, but rather he heard it directly from Christ. *Galatians 1:11-12* says, *"For I would have you know, brethren, that the gospel which was preached by me is not according to man. For I neither received it from man, nor was I taught it, but I received it through a revelation of Jesus Christ."* So, Paul heard and believed in Christ on the road to Damascus. Paul had already believed in Christ when Ananias came to pray for him to receive his sight (*Acts 9:17*).

It also should be noted that Paul at the time when Ananias prayed for him to receive his sight, he also received the Holy Spirit (*Acts 9:17*) this was before he was baptized (*Acts 9:18*). Acts presents a transition period where God's focus turns from Israel to the Church. The events recorded in Acts are not always normative. With regard to receiving the Holy Spirit, the norm is that a person receives and is permanently indwelt by the Holy Spirit at the moment of salvation.

The Greek aorist participle, epikalesamenos, translated "calling on His name" refers either to action that is simultaneous with or before that of the main verb, "be baptized." Here Paul's calling on Christ's name for salvation preceded his water baptism. The participle may be translated "having called on His name" which makes more sense, as it would clearly indicate the order of the events.

Concerning the words, "be baptized, and wash away your sins," because Paul was already cleansed spiritually at the time Christ appeared to him, these words must refer to the symbolism of baptism. Baptism is a picture of God's inner work of washing away sin (*1 Corinthians 6:11; 1 Peter 3:21*).

It is also interesting that when Paul recounted this event again later in *Acts* (*Acts 26:12-18*), he did not mention Ananias or what Ananias said to him at all. *Verse 18* again would confirm the idea that Paul received Christ as Savior on the road to Damascus since here Christ is telling Paul he will be a messenger for Him concerning forgiveness of sins for Gentiles as they have faith in Him. It would seem unlikely that Christ would commission Paul if Paul had not yet believed in Him.

Question: "Why is Christianity such a bloody religion?"

To understand why Christianity is a "bloody religion," we must go back to God's declarations regarding blood in the Old Testament: *"the life of the flesh is in the blood* (*Leviticus 17:11, 14*). Here God tells us that life and blood are essentially one and the same. The blood carries life-sustaining nutrients to all parts of the body. It represents the essence of life. In contrast, the shedding of blood represents the shedding of life, i.e. death.

Blood is also used in the Bible to represent spiritual life. When Adam and Eve sinned in the Garden of Eden by disobeying God and eating fruit of the forbidden tree, they experienced spiritual death immediately, and physical death years later. God's warning, *"You shall not eat of the tree of knowledge of good and evil. For in the day that you eat of it you shall surely die"* (*Genesis 2:17*) was fulfilled. Their blood, their lives, were now tainted by sin. In His gracious plan, however, God provided a "way out" of their dilemma by declaring that sacrifices of blood, first the blood of animals and finally the blood of the Lamb of God, Jesus Christ, would be sufficient to cover the sin of fallen mankind and restore us to spiritual life. He instituted the sacrificial system, beginning with the animals He himself killed to provide the first garments, thereby "covering" the sin of Adam and Eve (*Genesis 3:21*). All the Old Testament sacrifices which followed from then on were temporary ones, needing to be repeated over and over. These continual sacrifices were a foreshadowing of the one true and final sacrifice, Christ, whose blood would be shed on the cross and pay the penalty of sin forever. His death made any further bloodshed unnecessary (*Hebrews 10:1-10*).

As far as Christianity being a bloody religion, it is. But it is unique as a bloody religion. Contrary to bloodless religions, it takes sin seriously. This indicates that God takes sin seriously and gives a death penalty for it. Sin is not a small matter. It is the simple sin of pride that turned Lucifer into a demon. It was the simple sin of jealousy that caused Cain to slay Abel, etc. In Adam and Eve eating the forbidden fruit, they believed the deceiver over a good and loving God, choosing to rebel against His love and denying the goodness of His character. Christianity is a bloody religion because it views sin as a holy God views is … seriously.

Also, because God is just, sin requires a penalty. God cannot merely forgive in mercy until the demands of justice have been met. Thus the need for a sacrifice before forgiveness is possible. The shedding of the blood of animals, as Hebrews points out, could only "cover" sin for a time (*Hebrews 10:4*) until the intended and sufficient sacrifice was made in Christ's atoning death. Thus, Christianity is different from other bloody religions in that it alone provides a sufficient sacrifice to take care of the sin problem.

Last, although Christianity presents a bloody sacrifice in these regards, it is the only religion that is bloodless in the end. The opposite of death is life. In Jesus' death, He brought life as is shown in so many verses. And in trusting Christ and His atoning sacrifice for one's sins, one is saved from death and has passed into life (*John 5:24; 1 John 3:14*). In Him is life. All other paths lead to death (*Acts 4:16; John 14:6*).

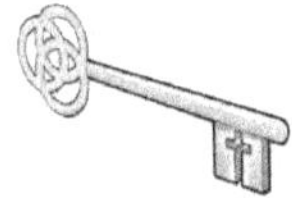

Question: "What does it mean to be a born again Christian?"

What does it mean to be a born again Christian? The classic passage from the Bible that answers this question is *John 3:1-21*. The Lord Jesus Christ is talking to Nicodemus, a prominent Pharisee and member of the Sanhedrin (a ruler of the Jews). Nicodemus had come to Jesus at night. Nicodemus had questions to ask Jesus.

As Jesus talked with Nicodemus, He said *"...Most assuredly, I say to you, unless one is born again, he cannot see the kingdom of God." Nicodemus said to Him, "How can a man be born when he is old? Can he enter a second time into his mother's womb and be born?" Jesus answered, "Most assuredly, I say to you, unless one is born of water and the Spirit, he cannot enter the kingdom of God. That which is born of the flesh is flesh, and that which is born of the Spirit is spirit. Do not marvel that I said to you, You must be born again...."* (*John 3:3-7*).

The phrase "born again" literally means "born from above." Nicodemus had a real need. He needed a change of his heart, a spiritual transformation. New birth, being born again, is an act of God whereby eternal life is imparted to the person who believes (*2 Corinthians 5:17; Titus 3:5; 1 Peter 1:3; 1 John 2:29; 3:9; 4:7; 5:1-4, 18*). *John 1:12 &*

13 indicates that "born again" also carries the idea "to become children of God" through trust in the name of Jesus Christ.

The question logically comes, "Why does a person need to be born again?" The Apostle Paul in *Ephesians 2:1* says, *"And you He made alive, who were dead in trespasses and sins..."* To the Romans in *Romans 3:23*, the Apostle wrote, *"For all have sinned and come short of the glory of God."* So, a person needs to be born again in order to have their sins forgiven and have a relationship with God.

How does that come to be? *Ephesians 2:8 & 9* states, *"For by grace you have been saved through faith, and that not of yourselves; it is the gift of God, not of works lest any man should boast."* When one is "saved," he/she has been born again, spiritually renewed, and is now a child of God by right of new birth. Trusting in Jesus Christ, the One who paid the penalty of sin when He died on the cross, is what it means to be "born again" spiritually. *"Therefore, if any man be in Christ, he is a new creation..."* (*2 Corinthians 5:17a*).

If you have never trusted in the Lord Jesus Christ as your Savior, will you consider the prompting of the Holy Spirit as He speaks to your heart? You need to be born again. Will you pray the prayer of repentance and become a new creation in Christ, today? *"But as many as received Him, to them He gave the right to become children of God, to those who believe on His name: who were born, not of blood, nor of the will of the flesh, nor of the will of man, but of God"* (*John 1:12-13*).

If you want to accept Jesus Christ as your Savior and be born again, here is a sample prayer. Remember, saying this prayer or any other prayer will not save you. It is only trusting in Christ that can save you from sin. This prayer is simply a way to express to God your faith in Him and thank Him for providing for your salvation. "God, I know that I have sinned against you and am deserving of punishment. But Jesus Christ took the punishment that I deserve so that through faith in Him I could be forgiven. I place my trust in You for salvation. Thank You for Your wonderful grace and forgiveness - the gift of eternal life! Amen!"

Question: "Why is the resurrection of Jesus Christ important?"

The resurrection of Jesus is important for several reasons. First, it witnesses to the immense power of God Himself. To believe in the resurrection is to believe in God. If God exists, and if He created the universe and has power over it, He has power to raise the dead. If He does not have such power, He is not a God worthy of our faith and worship. Only He who created life can resurrect it after death, only He can reverse the hideousness that is death itself, and only He can remove the sting that is death and the victory that is the graves. In resurrecting Jesus from the grave, God reminds us of His absolute sovereignty over life and death.

Second, the resurrection of Jesus is a testimony to the resurrection of human beings, which is a basic tenet of the Christian faith. Unlike all other religions, Christianity alone possesses a founder who transcends death and who promises that His followers will do the same. All other (false) religions were founded by men and prophets whose end was the grave. As Christians, we take comfort in the fact that our God became man, died for our sins, was killed, and was resurrected the third day. The grave could not hold Him. He lives and He sits today at the right hand of God the Father in heaven. The living church has a living Head.

In *1 Corinthians 15*, Paul explains in detail the importance of the resurrection of Christ. Some in Corinth did not believe in the resurrection of the dead, and in this chapter Paul gives six disastrous consequences if there were no resurrection:

1) preaching Christ would be senseless (*v. 14*);
2) faith in Christ would be useless (*v. 14*);
3) all the witnesses and preachers of the resurrection would be liars (*v. 15*);
4) no one would be redeemed from sin (*v. 17*);
5) all former believers would have perished (*v.18*) and
6) Christians would be the most pitiable people on the earth (*v. 19*).

But Christ indeed has risen from the dead and *"has become the first fruits of those who have fallen sleep"* (*v. 20*), assuring that we will follow Him in resurrection.

The inspired Word of God guarantees the believer's resurrection at the coming of Jesus Christ for His Body (the Church) at the Rapture. Such hope and assurance issues in a great song of triumph as Paul writes in *1 Corinthians 15:55, "O death, where is thy sting? O grave where is thy victory?"* How do these concluding verses relate to the importance of the Resurrection? Paul answers, *"...you know that your labor is not in vain"* (*v. 58*). He reminds us that because we know we will be resurrected to new life, we can suffer persecution and danger for Christ's sake (*vs. 29-31*), just as He did, and just as the thousands of martyrs through history who gladly traded their earthly lives for everlasting life via the resurrection.

The Resurrection is the triumphant and glorious victory for every believer in Jesus Christ who died, was buried, and rose the third day according to the Scripture. And, He is coming again! The dead in Christ will be raised up, and those who remain and are alive at His coming will be changed and receive new, glorified bodies (*1 Thessalonians 4:13-18*). Why is the resurrection of Jesus Christ important? It demonstrated that God accepted Jesus' sacrifice on our behalf. It proves that God has the power to raise us from the dead. It guarantees that those who believe in Christ will not remain dead, but will be resurrected unto eternal life. That is our blessed hope!

Question: "Will there be a second chance for salvation after death?"

While the idea of a second chance for salvation is appealing, the Bible is clear that death is the end of all chances. *Hebrews 9:27* tells us that we die, and then face judgment. So, as long as a person is alive, he has a second, third, fourth, fifth, etc. chance to accept Christ and be saved (*John 3:16; Romans 10:9-10; Acts 16:31*). Once a person dies, there are no more chances. The idea of purgatory, a place where people go after death to pay for their sins, has no biblical basis, but is rather a tradition of the Roman Catholic Church.

To understand what happens to nonbelievers after they die, we go to *Revelation 20:11-15* which describes the Great White Throne judgment. Here takes place the opening of the books and *"the dead were judged out of those things which were written in the books, according to their works."* The books contain all the thoughts and deeds of those being judged, and we know from *Romans 3:20* that *"by the works of the Law is no flesh justified."* Therefore, all who are judged by their works and thoughts are condemned to hell. Believers in Christ, on the other hand, are not judged by the books of works, but their names are found written in another book, the *"Lamb's Book of Life"* (*Revelation 21:27*). These are the ones who have believed on the Lord Jesus, and they alone will be allowed to enter heaven.

The key to understanding this is the Lamb's Book of Life. Anyone whose name is written in this book was *"saved before the foundation of the world"* (*Ephesians 1:4*) by God's sovereign saving grace to be part of His Son's bride, the church of Jesus Christ. These people need no "second chance" at salvation because their salvation has been secured by Christ. He chose us, He saved us, and He will keep us saved. Nothing can separate us from Christ (*Romans 8:39*). Those for whom He died will be saved because Jesus will see to it. He declared *"all that the Father has given me will come to me"* (*John 6:37*), and *"I give to them eternal life, and they shall never ever perish, and not anyone shall pluck them out of My hand"* (*John 10:28*). For believers, there is no need for a second chance because the first chance is sufficient.

What about those who do not believe? Wouldn't they repent and believe if they were given a second chance? The answer is no, they would not because their hearts are not changed simply because they die. Their hearts and minds "are at enmity" against God and won't accept Him even when they see Him face to face. This is evidenced clearly in the story of the rich man and Lazarus in *Luke 16:19-31*. If ever someone should have repented when given a second chance to see clearly the truth, it was the rich man. But although he was in torment in hell, he only asked that Abraham send Lazarus back to earth to warn his brothers so they didn't have to suffer the same fate. There was no repentance in his heart, only regret for where he found himself. Abraham's answer says it all: *"And he said to him, If they do not hear Moses and the Prophets, they will not be persuaded, even though one rose from the dead"* (*Luke 16:31*). Here we see that the witness of the Scriptures is sufficient for salvation for those who believe it, and no other revelation will bring about salvation to those who do not. No second, third or fourth chances would be enough to turn the heart of stone into a heart of flesh.

Philippians 2:10-11 declares *"that at the name of Jesus every knee should bow, in heaven and on earth and under the earth, and every tongue confess that Jesus Christ is Lord, to the glory of God the Father."* One day, everyone will bow before Jesus and recognize that He is the Lord and Savior. At that point, though, it is too late for salvation. After death, all that remains for the unbeliever is judgment (*Revelation 20:14-15*). That is why we must trust in Him in this life.

Question: "Do Christians have to keep asking for forgiveness for their sins?"

A frequent question is "what happens if I sin, and then I die before I have an opportunity to confess that sin to God?" Another common question is, "What happens if I commit a sin, but then forget about it, and never remember to confess it to God?" Both of these questions rest on a faulty assumption. Salvation is not a matter of believers trying to confess and repent from every sin they commit before they die. Salvation is not based on whether a Christian has confessed and repented of every sin. Yes, we should confess our sins to God as soon as we are aware that we have sinned. However, we do not always need to be asking God for forgiveness. When we place our faith in Jesus Christ for salvation, ALL of our sins are forgiven. That includes past, present, and future, big or small. Believers do not have to keep asking for forgiveness or repenting in order to have their sins forgiven. Jesus died to pay the penalty for all of our sins, and when they are forgiven, they are all forgiven (*Colossians 1:14; Acts 10:43*).

What we are to do is confess our sins: *"If we confess our sins, He is faithful and just and will forgive us our sins and purify us from all unrighteousness"* (*1 John 1:9*). Please note that this Scripture does not mention asking God for forgiveness. Scripture nowhere instructs believers in Christ to ask God for forgiveness. What *1 John 1:9* tells us to do is "confess" our sins to God. The word "confess" means "to agree with." When we confess our sins to God, we are agreeing with God that we were wrong, that we have sinned. God forgives us, through confession, on an ongoing basis because of the fact that He is "faithful and just." How is God "faithful and just?" He is faithful by forgiving sins; that He has promised to do for all those who receive Christ as Savior. He is just by applying Christ's payment for our sins, recognizing that the sins have indeed been atoned for.

1 John 1:9 does, though, indicate that somehow forgiveness is dependent on our confessing our sins to God. How does this work if all of our sins are forgiven the moment we receive Christ as Savior? It seems what the Apostle John is describing here is "relational" forgiveness. All of our sins are forgiven "positionally" the moment we receive Christ as Savior. This "positional" forgiveness guarantees our salvation and promise of an eternal home in Heaven. When we stand before God after death, God will not deny us entrance into Heaven because of our sins. That is "positional" forgiveness. The concept of "relational" forgiveness is based on the fact that when we sin, we offend God and grieve His Spirit (*Ephesians 4:30*). While God has ultimately forgiven us of the sins we commit, they still result in a blocking or hindrance in our relationship with God. A young boy who sins against his father is not cast out of the family. A godly father will forgive his children unconditionally. At the same time, a good relationship between father and son cannot be achieved until the relationship is restored. This can only occur when a child confesses his mistakes to his father, and apologizes. That is why we confess our sins to God…not to maintain our salvation, but to bring ourselves back into close fellowship with the God who loves us and has already forgiven us.

Question: "What is the sinner's prayer?"

The sinner's prayer is a prayer a person prays to God when they understand that they are a sinner and in need of a Savior. Saying a sinner's prayer will not accomplish anything on its own. A sinner's prayer is only effective if it genuinely represents what a person knows, understands, and believes about their sinfulness and need for salvation.

The first aspect of a sinner's prayer is understanding that we are all sinners. *Romans 3:10* proclaims, *"As it is written, There is none righteous, no, not one."* The Bible makes it clear that we have all sinned. We are all sinners in need of mercy and forgiveness from God (*Titus*

3:5-7). Because of our sin, we deserve eternal punishment (*Matthew 25:46*). The sinner's prayer is a plea for grace instead of judgment. It is a request for mercy instead of wrath.

The second aspect of a sinner's prayer is knowing what God has done to remedy our lost and sinful condition. God took on flesh and became a human being in the Person of Jesus Christ (*John 1:1,14*). Jesus taught us the truth about God and lived a perfectly righteous and sinless life (*John 8:46; 2 Corinthians 5:21*). Jesus then died on the cross in our place, taking the punishment that we deserve (*Romans 5:8*). Jesus rose from the dead to prove His victory over sin, death, and hell (*Colossians 2:15; 1 Corinthians 15*). Because of all of this, we can have our sins forgiven and be promised an eternal home in Heaven - if we will just place our faith in Jesus Christ. All we have to do is believe that He died in our place and rose from the dead (*Romans 10:9-10*). We can be saved by grace alone, through faith alone, in Jesus Christ alone. *Ephesians 2:8* declares, *"For it is by grace you have been saved, through faith - and this not from yourselves, it is the gift of God."*

Saying the sinner's prayer is simply a way of declaring to God that you are relying on Jesus Christ as your Savior. There are no "magical" words that result in salvation. It is only faith in Jesus' death and resurrection that can save us. If you understand that you are a sinner and in need of salvation through Jesus Christ, here is a sinner's prayer you can pray to God: "God, I know that I am a sinner. I know that I deserve the consequences of my sin. However, I am trusting in Jesus Christ as my Savior. I believe that His death and resurrection provided for my forgiveness. I trust in Jesus and Jesus alone as my personal Lord and Savior. Thank you Lord, for saving me and forgiving me! Amen!"

Question: "If you doubt your salvation, does that mean you are not truly saved?"

Everyone has occasional doubts. Whether or not you have doubts is not what determines whether you are a Christian. Even when a believer is faithless, God is faithful (*2 Timothy 2:13*). God wants us to be sure and confident of our salvation (*Romans 8:38-39; 1 John 5:13*). God promises that everyone who believes in Jesus Christ will be saved (*John 3:16; Romans 10:9-10*). We have all sinned and fallen short of God's glory (*Romans 3:23*). As a result, we deserve death and an eternity apart from God (*Romans 6:23*). But God loved us enough to die in our place, taking the punishment that we deserved (*Romans 5:8*). As a result, all those who believe are saved and eternally secure.

Sometimes doubting is a good thing. Paul tells us in *2 Corinthians 13:5 "examine yourselves as to whether you are in the faith."* We are to test ourselves to be sure that Jesus is truly our Savior and the Holy Spirit is truly in us. If He is, we can in no way lose the salvation Christ has obtained for us (*Romans 8:38-39*). If He's not, then perhaps the Holy Spirit is convicting us of sin and prompting us to repent and be reconciled to God through Christ. The assurance of our salvation comes from the knowledge that once we are in Christ, we are eternally secure. But genuine saving faith is evidenced by its works (*James 2:14-26*) and the fruit of the Spirit within us (*Galatians 5:22*). The lack of this evidence can sometimes be the cause of our doubts.

Have you placed your faith in Christ? If the answer is yes, then throw away your doubts and trust God. If you know Jesus as your Savior, you are saved without a doubt! If the answer is no, then believe in the Lord Jesus Christ and you will be saved!

Question: "Where do I find the age of accountability in the Bible? What happens to babies and young children when they die?"

The Bible tells us that even if an infant or child has not committed personal sin, all people, including infants and children, are guilty before God because of inherited and imputed sin. Inherited sin is that which is passed on from our parents. In *Psalm 51:5*, David wrote, *"I was brought forth in iniquity, and in sin my mother conceived me."* David recognized that even at conception, he was a sinner. The very sad fact that infants sometimes die demonstrates that even infants are impacted by Adam's sin, since physical and spiritual death were the results of Adam's original sin.

Each person, infant or adult, stands guilty before God; each person has offended the holiness of God. The only way that God can be just and at the same time declare a person righteous is for that person to have received forgiveness by faith in Christ. Christ is the only way. *John 14:6* records what Jesus said, *"I am the way, and the truth, and the life; no one comes to the Father, but through Me."* Also, Peter stated in *Acts 4:12*, *"there is salvation in no one else; for there is no other name under heaven that has been given among men, by which we must be saved."* Salvation is an individual choice.

What about babies and young children who never reach the ability to make this individual choice? The "age of accountability" is a concept that teaches those who die before reaching the "age of accountability" are automatically saved, by God's grace and mercy. Thirteen is the most common number given for the age of accountability based on the Jewish custom that a child becomes an adult at the age of 13. However, the Bible gives no direct support to the age of 13 always being the age of accountability. It likely varies from child to child. A child has passed the age of accountability once he or she is capable of making a faith decision for or against Christ.

With the above in mind, also consider the following: Christ's death is presented as sufficient for all of mankind. *1 John 2:2* says Jesus *"is the propitiation for our sins; and not for ours only, but also for those of the whole world."* This verse is clear that Jesus' death was sufficient for all sins, not just the sins of those who specifically have come to Him in faith. The fact that Christ's death was sufficient for all sin would allow the possibility of God applying that payment to those who were never capable of believing.

The one passage that seems to identify with this topic more than any other is *2 Samuel 12:21-23*. The context of these verses is that King David committed adultery with Bathsheba, with a resulting pregnancy. The prophet Nathan was sent by the Lord to inform David that because of his sin, the Lord would take the child in death. David responded to this by grieving, mourning, and praying for the child. But, once the child was taken, David's mourning ended. David's servants were surprised to hear this. They said to King David, *"What is this thing that you have done? While the child was alive, you fasted and wept; but when the child died, you arose and ate food." David's response was, "While the child was still alive, I fasted and wept; for I said, 'Who knows, the LORD may be gracious to me, that the child may live.' But now he has died; why should I fast? Can I bring him back again? I shall go to him, but he will not return to me."* David's response can be seen as an argument that those who cannot believe are safe in the Lord. David said that he could go to the child, but that he could not bring the child back to him. Also, and just as important, David seemed to be comforted over this. In other words, David seemed to be saying that he would once again see the child (in heaven), though he could not bring him back.

Though the Bible leaves open the possibility, the one problem with saying that God applies Christ's payment for sin to those who can't believe is that the Bible does not specifically say that He does this. Therefore, this is a subject for which we should not be adamant or dogmatic. We can, however, be dogmatic about the fact that God ALWAYS does what is right.

Knowing the love and grace of God, God applying Christ's death to those who cannot believe would seem consistent with His character. It is our position that God applies Christ's payment for sin to young children and those who are mentally handicapped, since they were not mentally capable of understanding their sinful state and their need for the Savior. Of this we are certain, that God is loving, holy, merciful, just, and gracious. Whatever He does, it is ALWAYS right and good.

Question: "Does God forgive big sins? Will God forgive a murderer?"

Many people make the mistake of believing that God forgives "little" sins such as lying, anger, and impure thoughts, but does not forgive "big" sins such as murder and adultery. This is not true. There is no sin too big that God cannot forgive it. When Jesus died on the cross, He died to pay the penalty for all of the sins of the entire world (*1 John 2:2*). When a person places his faith in Jesus Christ for salvation, all of his sins are forgiven. That includes past, present, and future, big or small. Jesus died to pay the penalty for all of our sins, and once they are forgiven, they are all forgiven (*Colossians 1:14; Acts 10:43*).

We are all guilty of sin (*Romans 3:23*) and deserve eternal punishment (*Romans 6:23*). Jesus died for us, to pay our penalty (*Romans 5:8*). Anyone who believes in Jesus Christ for salvation is forgiven, no matter what sins he has committed (*Romans 6:23; John 3:16*). Now, a murderer or adulterer will likely still face serious consequences (legal, relational, etc.) for his evil actions; more so than someone who was "just" a liar. But a murderer's or adulterer's sins are completely and permanently forgiven the moment he believes and places his faith in Christ.

It is not the size of the sin that is the determining factor here; it is the size of the atoning sacrifice of Christ. If the shed blood of the sinless Lamb of God is sufficient to cover all the sins of all the millions of people who would ever believe in Him, then there can be no limit to the size or types of sins covered. When He said, "It is finished," sin was made an end of, full atonement and satisfaction for it were given, complete pardon was obtained, peace was made, and redemption from all sin was achieved. It was sure and certain and complete; nothing needs to be, or could be, added to it. Further, it was done entirely without the help of man, and cannot be undone.

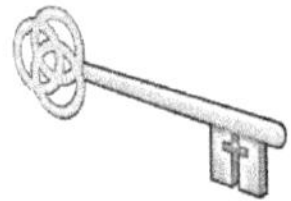

Question: "How does God's sovereignty and mankind's free will work together in salvation?"

It is impossible for us to fully understand the relationship between God's sovereignty and man's free will. Only God truly knows how those two work together.

Scripture is clear that God knows who will be saved (*Romans 8:29; 1 Peter 1:2*). *Ephesians 1:4* tells us that God chose us *"before the foundation of the world."* The Bible repeatedly describes believers as the "chosen" (*Romans 8:33; 11:5; Ephesians 1:11; Colossians 3:12; 1 Thessalonians 1:4; 1 Peter 1:2; 2:9*) and the "elect" (*Matthew 24:22, 31; Mark 13:20, 27; Romans 11:7; 1 Timothy 5:21; 2 Timothy 2:10; Titus 1:1; 1 Peter 1:1*). The fact that believers are predestined (*Romans 8:29-30; Ephesians 1:5, 11*) and elected (*Romans 9:11; 11:28; 2 Peter 1:10*) for salvation is plainly clear.

The Bible also says that we have the free will choice – all we have to do is believe in Jesus Christ and we will be saved (*John 3:16; Romans 10:9-10*). God knows who will be saved, God chooses who will be saved, and we must choose Christ in order to be saved. How these three facts work together is impossible for a finite mind to comprehend (*Romans 11:33-36*). Our responsibility is to take the Gospel to the whole world (*Matthew 28:18-20; Acts 1:8*). We should leave the foreknowledge, election, and predestination part up to God and simply be obedient in sharing the Gospel.

Question: "Why did Jesus have to die?"

When we ask a question such as this, we must be careful that we are not calling God into question. To wonder why God couldn't find "another way" to do something is to imply that the way He has chosen is not the best course of action and that some other method would be better. Usually what we perceive as a "better" method is one that seems right to us. Before we can come to grips with anything God does, we have to first acknowledge that His ways are not our ways, His thoughts are not our thought; they are higher than ours (*Isaiah 55:8*). In addition *Deuteronomy 32:4* reminds us that *"He is the Rock, his works are perfect, and all his ways are just. A faithful God who does no wrong, upright and just is he."* Therefore, the plan of salvation He has designed is perfect, just, and upright, no one could have come up with anything better.

The Scripture says, *"For I delivered to you as of first importance what I also received: that Christ died for our sins in accordance with the Scriptures, that he was buried, that he was raised on the third day in accordance with the Scriptures"* (*1 Corinthians 15:3-4*). Evidence affirms that the sinless Jesus bled and died on a cross. Most importantly, the Bible explains why Jesus' death and resurrection provide the only entrance to heaven.

- **The punishment for sin is death -** God created earth and man perfect. But when Adam and Eve disobeyed God's commands, He had to punish them. A judge who pardons law-breakers isn't a righteous judge. Likewise, overlooking sin would make the holy God unjust. Death is God's just consequence for sin. *"For the wages of sin is death"* (*Romans 6:23*). Even good works cannot make up for wrongs against the holy God. Compared to His goodness, *"All our righteousnesses are as filthy rags"* (*Isaiah 64:6b*). Ever since Adam's sin, every human has been guilty of disobeying God's righteous laws. *"For all have sinned and fall short of the glory of God"* (*Romans 3:23*). Sin is not just big things like murder or blasphemy, but also includes love of money, hatred of enemies, and deceit of tongue and pride. Because of sin, everyone has deserved death; eternal separation from God in hell.

- **The promise required an innocent death -** Although God banished Adam and Eve from the garden, He didn't leave them without hope of heaven. He promised He would send a sinless Sacrifice to take the punishment they deserved (*Genesis 3:15*). Until then, men would sacrifice innocent lambs, showing their repentance from sin and faith in the future Sacrifice from God who would bear their penalty. God reaffirmed His promise of the Sacrifice with men such as Abraham and Moses. Herein lies the beauty of God's perfect plan: God Himself provided the only sacrifice (Jesus) who could atone for the sins of His people. God's perfect Son fulfilled God's perfect requirement of God's perfect law. It is perfectly brilliant in its simplicity. *"God made Him (Christ), who knew no sin, to be sin for us that we might become the righteousness of God in Him"* (*2 Corinthians 5:21*).
- **The prophets foretold Jesus' death -** From Adam to Jesus, God sent prophets to mankind, warning them of sin's punishment and foretelling the coming Messiah. One prophet, Isaiah, described Him:
    - *"Who has believed what they heard from us? And to whom has the arm of the LORD been revealed? For he grew up before him like a young plant, and like a root out of dry ground; he had no form or majesty that we should look at him, and no beauty that we should desire him. He was despised and rejected by men; a man of sorrows, and acquainted with grief; and as one from whom men hide their faces he was despised, and we esteemed him not. Surely he has borne our griefs and carried our sorrows; yet we esteemed him stricken, smitten by God, and afflicted. But he was wounded for our transgressions; he was crushed for our iniquities; upon him was the chastisement that brought us*

peace, and with his stripes we are healed. All we like sheep have gone astray; we have turned every one to his own way; and the LORD has laid on him the iniquity of us all. He was oppressed, and he was afflicted, yet he opened not his mouth; like a lamb that is led to the slaughter, and like a sheep that before its shearers is silent, so he opened not his mouth. By oppression and judgment he was taken away; and as for his generation, who considered that he was cut off out of the land of the living, stricken for the transgression of my people? And they made his grave with the wicked and with a rich man in his death, although he had done no violence, and there was no deceit in his mouth. Yet it was the will of the LORD to crush him; he has put him to grief; when his soul makes an offering for sin, he shall see his offspring; he shall prolong his days; the will of the LORD shall prosper in his hand. Out of the anguish of his soul he shall see and be satisfied; by his knowledge shall the righteous one, my servant, make many to be accounted righteous, and he shall bear their iniquities. Therefore I will divide him a portion with the many, and he shall divide the spoil with the strong, because he poured out his soul to death and was numbered with the transgressors; yet he bore the sin of many, and makes intercession for the transgressors" (*Isaiah 53:1-12*).

He likened the coming Sacrifice to a lamb, slaughtered for the sins of others. Hundreds of years later, Isaiah's prophecy was fulfilled in the perfect Lord Jesus, born of the virgin Mary. When the prophet John the Baptist saw Him, he cried, *"Behold, the Lamb of God, who takes away the sin of the world!"* (*John 1:29*). Crowds thronged Him for healing and teaching, but the religious leaders scorned Him. Mobs cried out, "Crucify Him!" Soldiers beat, mocked, and crucified Him. As Isaiah foretold, Jesus was crucified in between two criminals but was buried in a rich man's tomb. But He didn't remain in the grave. Because God accepted His Lamb's sacrifice, He fulfilled another prophecy by raising Jesus from the dead (*Psalm 16:10; Isaiah 26:19*).

- **Why did Jesus have to die -** Remember, the holy God cannot let sin go unpunished. To bear our own sins would be to suffer God's judgment in the flames of hell. Praise God, He kept His promise to send and sacrifice the perfect Lamb to bear the sins of those who trust in Him. Jesus had to die because He is the only one who can pay the penalty for our sins.

Question: "Do mentally ill people go to heaven? Does God show mercy to those who are mentally retarded, challenged, disabled, or handicapped?"

The Bible does not specifically say whether or not mentally ill people go to heaven. However, there is some biblical evidence that anyone who is not able to make a decision for salvation is covered by Christ's death. This is similar to how it is commonly believed that children are automatically taken to heaven when they die until they reach the point in which they are able to make a decision for or against Christ. David had a child die, and he comforted himself with the thought, *"Can I bring him back again? I will go to him, but he will not return to me"* (*2 Samuel 12:23*). David knew that he would see his child in heaven one day. From that statement, we can assume that babies and young children were, by God's grace, covered for salvation by Christ's death.

We can postulate from this that mentally retarded people are covered by this principle as well. The Word of God does not specifically say this, however. Knowing the love, grace, and mercy of God, this would seem consistent with His character. Any person who is mentally challenged to the extent that he could not be aware of his sinful state and believe in Christ for salvation, is in the same category as a child and it is not unreasonable to assume that person is saved by the grace and mercy of the same God who saves babies and small children.

As in everything, however, we must be careful not to be dogmatic about any issue the Bible does not specifically address. We do know that Jesus receives as His own all that the Father has given to Him and He will lose none of them along the way (*John 6:39*). Jesus said of these *"And I give to them eternal life, and they shall never ever perish, and not anyone shall pluck them out of My hand"* (*John 10:28*). We can take comfort in knowing that our God's plan is always perfect, He always does what is right and just, and His love and mercy are infinite and everlasting.

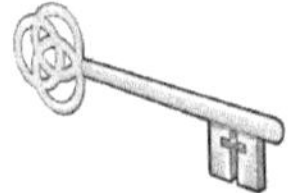

Question: "Does *Hebrews 6:4-6* mean we can lose our salvation?"

Hebrews 6:4-6 states, *"For it is impossible for those who were once enlightened, and have tasted the heavenly gift, and have become partakers of the Holy Spirit, and have tasted the good word of God and the powers of the age to come, if they fall away, to renew them again to repentance, since they crucify again for themselves the Son of God, and put Him to an open shame."* This is one of the Bible's most difficult passages to interpret. But one thing is clear, it does not teach that we can lose our salvation. There are two valid ways of looking at these verses.

One interpretation holds that this passage is written not about Christians but about unbelievers who are convinced of the basic truths of the gospel but who have not placed their faith in Jesus Christ as Savior. They are intellectually persuaded but spiritually uncommitted.

According to this interpretation, the phrase *"once enlightened"* (*verse 4*) refers to some level of instruction in biblical truth. However, understanding the words of scripture is not the same as being regenerated by the Holy Spirit. For example, *John 1:9* describes Jesus, the *"true Light,"* giving light *"to every man"*; but this cannot mean the light of salvation, because not every man is saved. Through God's sovereign power, every man has enough light to be held responsible. This light either leads to the complete acceptance of Jesus Christ or produces condemnation in those who reject such light. The people described in *Hebrews 6:4-6* are of the latter group, unbelievers who have been exposed to God's redemptive truth and perhaps have made a profession of faith, but have not exercised genuine saving faith.

This interpretation also sees the phrase *"tasted the heavenly gift"* (*Hebrews 6:9*) as referring to a momentary experience, akin to Jesus' "tasting" death (*Hebrews 2:9*). This brief experience with the heavenly gift is not seen as equivalent to salvation; rather, it is likened to the second and third soils in Jesus' parable (*Matthew 13:3-23*), which describes people who receive the truth of the gospel but are not truly saved.

Finally, this interpretation sees the *"falling away"* (*Hebrews 6:6*) as a reference to those who have tasted the truth but, not having come all the way to faith, fall away from even the revelation they have been given. The tasting of truth is not enough to keep them from falling away from it. They must come all the way to Christ in complete repentance and faith; otherwise, they in effect re-crucify Christ and treat Him contemptuously. Those who sin against Christ in such a way have no hope of restoration or forgiveness because they reject Him with full knowledge and conscious experience. They have concluded that Jesus should have been crucified, and they stand with His enemies. It is impossible to renew such to repentance.

The other interpretation holds that this passage is written about Christians, and that the phrases *"partakers of the Holy Ghost," "enlightened,"* and *"tasted of the heavenly gift"* are all descriptions of true believers.

According to this interpretation, the key word in the passage is if (*verse 6*). The writer of *Hebrews* is setting up a hypothetical statement: *"IF a Christian were to fall away . . ."* The point being made is that it would be impossible (*IF a Christian falls away*) to renew salvation. That's because Christ died once for sin (*Hebrews 9:28*), and if His sacrifice is insufficient, then there's no hope at all.

The passage, therefore, presents an argument based on a false premise (that a true Christian can fall away) and follows it to its senseless conclusion (that Jesus would have to be sacrificed again and again). The absurdity of the conclusion points up the impossibility of the original assumption. This reasoning is called reductio ad absurdum, in which a premise is disproved by showing that it logically leads to an absurdity.

Both of these interpretations support the security of the believer in Christ. The first interpretation presents unbelievers rejecting Christ and thereby losing their chance of salvation; the second interpretation presents the very idea of believers losing salvation as impossible. Many scriptures make it abundantly clear that salvation is eternal (*John 10:27 -29; Romans 8:35, 38-39; Philippians 1:6; 1 Peter 1:4-5*), and *Hebrews 6:4-6* confirms that doctrine.

Question: "Does *Hebrews 10:26* mean that a believer can lose salvation?"

"For if we are willfully sinning after receiving the full knowledge of the truth, there remains no more sacrifice concerning sins." Hebrews

10:26-29 warns against the sin of apostasy. Apostasy is an intentional falling away or defection. Apostates are those who move toward Christ, right up to the edge of saving belief, who hear and understand the Gospel, and are on the verge of saving faith, but then reject what they have learned and turn away. These are people who are perhaps even aware of their sin and even make a profession of faith. But rather than going on to spiritual maturity, their interest in Christ begins to diminish, the things of the world have more attraction to them rather than less, and eventually they lose all desire for the things of God and they turn away. The Lord illustrated these types of people in the second and third soils of *Matthew 13:1-9, 18-23*. These are those who *"receive with joy"* the things of the Lord, but who are drawn away by the cares of the world or turned off by difficulties they encounter because of Christ.

"Willful sinning" in this passage carries the idea of consciously and deliberately rejecting Christ. To know God's way, to hear it preached, to study it, to count oneself among the faithful, and then to turn away is to become apostate. Sinning willfully carries with it the idea of sinning continually and deliberately. Such a person does not sin because of ignorance, nor is he carried away by momentary temptations he is too weak to resist. The willful sinner sins because of an established way of thinking and acting which he has no desire to give up. The true believer, on the other hand, is one who lapses into sin and loses temporary fellowship with God. But he will eventually come back to God in repentance because his heavenly Father will continually woo and convict him until he can't stay away any longer. The true apostate will continue to sin, deliberately, willingly and with abandon. John tells us that *"No one who is born of God practices sin, because His seed abides in him and he cannot sin, because he is born of God"* (*1 John 3:9*).

Apostates have knowledge, but no application of that knowledge. They can be found in the presence of the light of Christ, mostly in the church, among God's people. Judas Iscariot is the perfect example, he had knowledge but he lacked true faith. No other rejector of the truth had more or better exposure to the love and grace of God than Judas. He was part of Jesus' inner circle of disciples, eating, sleeping, and traveling with Him for years. He saw the miracles and heard the words of God from Jesus' very lips, from the best preacher the world has ever known, and yet he not only turned away but was instrumental in the plot to kill Jesus.

Having turned his back on the truth, and with full knowledge choosing to willfully and continually sin, the apostate is then beyond salvation because he has rejected the one true sacrifice for sins: the Lord Jesus Christ. If Christ's sacrifice is rejected, then all hope of salvation is gone. To turn away willfully from this sacrifice leaves no sacrifice; it leaves only sin, the penalty for which is eternal death. This passage is not speaking of a believer who falls away, but rather someone who may claim to be a believer, but truly is not. Anyone who apostatizes is proving he never had genuine faith to begin with (*1 John 2:19*).

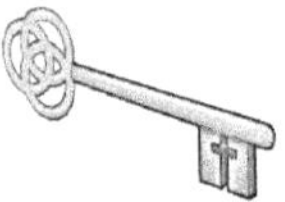

Question: "What is sanctification? What is the definition of Christian sanctification?"

Jesus had a lot to say about sanctification in the *Book of John, chapter 17*. In *verse 16* the Lord says, *"They are not of the world, even as I am not of the world,"* and this is before His request: *"Sanctify them in the truth: Thy word is truth."* Sanctification is a state of separation unto God; all believers enter into this state when they are born of God: *"But of Him you are in Christ Jesus, who became for us wisdom from God—and righteousness and sanctification and redemption"* (*1 Corinthians 1:30*). This is a once-for-ever separation, eternally unto God. It is an intricate part of our salvation, our connection with Christ (*Hebrews 10:10*).

Sanctification also refers to the practical experience of this separation unto God, being the effect of obedience to the Word of God in one's life, and is to be pursued by the believer earnestly (*1 Peter 1:15; Hebrews 12:14*). Just as the Lord prayed in *John 17*, it has in view the setting apart of believers for the purpose for which they are sent into the world: *"As Thou didst send Me into the world, even so send I them into the world. And for their sakes I sanctify Myself, that they themselves also may be sanctified in truth"* (*v. 18, 19*). That He set Himself apart for the purpose for which He was sent is both the basis and the condition of our being set apart for that for which we are sent (*John 10:36*). His sanctification is the pattern of, and the power for, ours. The sending and the sanctifying are inseparable. On this account they are called saints, hagioi in the Greek; "sanctified ones." Whereas previously their behavior bore witness to their standing in the world in separation from God, now their behavior should bear witness to their standing before God in separation from the world.

There is one more sense that the word sanctification is referred to in Scripture. Paul prayed in *1 Thessalonians 5:23*, *"The God of peace Himself sanctify you wholly; and may your spirit and soul and body be preserved entire, without blame at the coming of our Lord Jesus Christ."* Paul also wrote in Colossians of *"the hope which is laid up for you in the heavens, whereof ye heard before in the word of the truth of the Gospel"* (*Colossians 1:5*). He later speaks of Christ Himself as *"the hope of glory"* (*Colossians 1:27*) and then mentions the fact of that hope when he says, *"When Christ, who is our Life, shall be manifested, then shall ye also with Him be manifested in glory"* (*Colossians 3:4*). This glorified state will be our ultimate separation from sin, total sanctification in every aspect. *"Beloved, now we are children of God; and it has not yet been revealed what we shall be, but we know that when He is revealed, we shall be like Him, for we shall see Him as He is"* (*1 John 3:2*).

To summarize, sanctification is the same Greek word as holiness, "hagios," meaning a separation. First, a once-for-all positional separation unto Christ at our salvation. Second, a practical progressive holiness in a believer's life while awaiting the return of Christ. Third, we will be changed into His perfect likeness; holy, sanctified, and completely separated from the presence of evil.

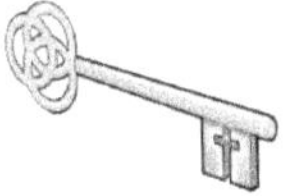

Question: "Why did God require animal sacrifices in the Old Testament?"

God required animal sacrifices so that mankind could receive forgiveness for their sins (*Leviticus 4:35; 5:10*). To begin, animal sacrifice is an important theme found throughout Scripture. When Adam and Eve sinned, animals were killed by God to provide clothing for them (*Genesis 3:21*). Cain and Abel brought sacrifices to the Lord. Cain's was unacceptable because he brought fruit, while Abel's was acceptable because it was the *"firstlings of his flock"* (*Genesis 4:4-5*). After the flood receded, Noah sacrificed animals to God. This sacrifice from Noah was an aroma that was soothing to the Lord (*Genesis 8:20-21*). God commanded Abraham to sacrifice his son Isaac. Abraham obeyed God, but just as Abraham was to sacrifice Isaac, God intervened and provided a ram to die in the place of Isaac (*Genesis 22:10-13*).

The sacrificial system reaches its climax with the nation of Israel. God commanded the nation to perform numerous different sacrifices. According to *Leviticus 1:1-4*, a certain procedure was to be followed. First, the animal had to be spotless. Next, the person offering the sacrifice had to identify with the animal. Then the person offering the animal had to inflict death upon it. When done in faith, this sacrifice provided forgiveness of sins. Another sacrifice called the day of atonement, described in *Leviticus 16*, demonstrates forgiveness and the removal of sin. The high priest was to take two male goats for a sin offering. One of the goats was sacrificed as a sin offering for the people of Israel (*Leviticus 16:15*), while the other goat was released into the wilderness (*Leviticus 16:20-22*). The sin offering provided forgiveness, while the other goat provided the removal of sin.

Why, then, do we no longer offer animal sacrifices today? Animal sacrifices have ended because Jesus Christ was the ultimate sacrifice. John the Baptist recognized this when he saw Jesus for the first time, *"Behold, the lamb of God who takes away the sin of the world"* (*John 1:29*). You may be asking yourself, why animals? What did they do wrong? That is the point, in that since the animals did no wrong, they died in place of the one performing the sacrifice. Jesus Christ also knew no wrong but willingly gave Himself to die for the sins of mankind (*1 Timothy 2:6*). Many people call this idea of dying in place of someone else substitution. Jesus Christ took our sin upon himself and died in our place. As *2 Corinthians 5:21* says, *"He (God) made Him (Jesus) who knew no sin to be sin on our behalf, that we might become the righteousness of God in Him."* Through faith in what Jesus Christ accomplished on the cross, the individual can receive forgiveness.

In summation, the animal sacrifices were commanded by God so that the individual could experience forgiveness of his sins. The animal served as a substitute; that is, the animal died in place of the sinner. Animal sacrifices have stopped with Jesus Christ. Jesus Christ was the ultimate sacrificial substitute and is now the only mediator between God and mankind (*1 Timothy 2:5*). Animal sacrifices foreshadowed Christ's sacrifice on our behalf. The only basis on which an animal sacrifice could provide forgiveness of sins is the fact that Christ would sacrifice Himself for our sins, providing the forgiveness that animal sacrifices could only illustrate and foreshadow.

Question: "How young can you be and ask Jesus to be your Savior?"

There is definitely no age requirement for salvation. Jesus Himself declared, *"Let the little children come to me, and do not hinder them, for the kingdom of heaven belongs to such as these"* (*Matthew 19:14*).

As soon as children are old enough to understand that they have sinned (*Romans 3:23*), that Jesus died to pay the penalty for their sins (*Romans 5:8; 6:23*), and that they must place their faith in Jesus for salvation (*John 3:16*), then they are old enough to be saved.

A child does not have to understand all the complex issues that are part of the doctrine of salvation. The Bible often encourages us to have faith like a child (*Matthew 18:4; Mark 10:15; Luke 18:17*). It is important that parents make sure that their children understand the basic issues, as described above. But the promise of *Acts 16:31* is equally true with regard to an adult or a child: *"Believe in the Lord Jesus, and you will be saved."*

Little children, whether born of believers or unbelievers, may be chosen of God, redeemed by the blood of Christ, and have the work of the Holy Spirit in their hearts, and so enter into heaven. At what point in their lives they come to a realization of these things will vary from child to child.

Some young children have especially tender hearts and, upon hearing that Jesus died for them, are immediately aware of their sinful natures and are compelled to respond. Others of more sanguine personalities may not come to this awareness until they are much older. Only the Lord knows the thoughts of the heart and we trust Him *"to seek and save that which is lost" (Luke 19:10)* according to His perfect will and timing.

Question: "Can a child who is conceived out of wedlock be saved?"

In *Deuteronomy 23:2*, the Mosaic Law says, *"The child begotten out of wedlock or incest shall not enter into the congregation of the Lord; even to his tenth generation shall he not enter into the congregation of the Lord."* What this was saying is the child born out of wedlock was illegitimate and unworthy of Israelite citizenship for ten generations. This does not mean, as some mistakenly think, that an illegitimate person cannot be saved or be used greatly by God. His mercy and grace through Christ are sufficient for all.

In the New Testament, *Hebrews 12:8* mentions *"But if you are without correction, where all are partakers, then are you bastards, and not sons."* This is telling us that whom the Lord loves He chastens, and corrects every child of His. Those He does not correct and discipline are not really His children, and therefore, will not enter the Kingdom of Heaven. We must be one of God's own, born from above, to enter into Heaven.

So we can clearly see that anyone who trusts Jesus Christ as his or her personal Savior will enter the Kingdom of Heaven. *John 3:16-18* says it all, *"For God so loved the world, that He gave His only begotten Son, that whosoever believes in Him should not perish, but have everlasting life. For God sent not his Son into the world to condemn the world, but that the world through Him might be saved. He that believes on him is not condemned; but he that believes not is condemned already, because he has not believed in the name of the only begotten Son of God."*

When God looks down on His children who have received that free gift of salvation through the death, burial, and resurrection of Jesus Christ, He does not see our nationality, color, legitimacy or non-legitimacy of birth, only the righteousness of Christ in us (*2 Corinthians 5:21; Philippians 3:9*). We are not saved because of who we are from birth; rather, we are saved because of who we become at the new birth. We become new creations in Christ. *"Therefore, if anyone is in Christ, he is a new creation; old things have passed away; behold, all things have become new"* (*2 Corinthians 5:17*). When a child born out of wedlock is born again, he/she becomes a son or daughter of the living God (*John 1:12*).

In *Psalm 139* David is praising God for *"You shaped me first inside, then out; You formed me in my mother's womb. I thank you, High God - you're breathtaking! Body and soul, I am marvelously made! I worship in adoration - what a creation! You know me inside and out, you know every bone in my body; You know exactly how I was made, bit by bit, how I was sculpted from nothing into something. Like an open book, you watched me grow from conception to birth; all the stages of my life were spread out before you. The days of my life all prepared before I'd even lived one day. Your thoughts - how rare, how beautiful! God, I'll never comprehend them!"* Our marvelous Creator loves all the little fetuses, no matter the state of conception, and has through His grace, provided a home in heaven for all who will receive that free gift of salvation. Praise the Lord!

Question: "What is repentance and is it necessary for salvation?"

Many understand the term "repentance" to mean "turning from sin." This is not the Biblical definition of repentance. In the Bible, the word "repent" means to "change your mind." The Bible also tells us that true repentance will result in a change of actions (*Luke 3:8-14; Acts 3:19*). *Acts 26:20* declares, *"I preached that they should repent and turn to God and prove their repentance by their deeds."* The full Biblical definition of repentance is a change of mind that results in a change of action.

What, then, is the connection between repentance and salvation? The *Book of Acts* seems to especially focus on repentance in regards to salvation (*Acts 2:38; 3:19; 11:18; 17:30; 20:21; 26:20*). To repent, in relation to salvation, is to change your mind in regards to Jesus Christ. In Peter's sermon on the Day of Pentecost (*Acts 2*), he concludes with a call for the people to repent (*Acts 2:38*). Repent from what? Peter is calling the people who rejected Jesus (*Acts 2:36*) to change their minds about Him, to recognize that He is indeed *"Lord and Christ"* (*Acts 2:36*). Peter is calling the people to change their minds from rejection of Christ as the Messiah, to faith in Him as both Messiah and Savior.

Repentance and faith can be understood as *"two sides of the same coin."* It is impossible to place your faith in Jesus Christ as the Savior without first changing your mind about who He is and what He has done. Whether it is repentance from willful rejection or repentance from ignorance or disinterest, it is a change of mind. Biblical repentance, in relation to salvation, is changing your mind from rejection of Christ, to faith in Christ.

It is crucially important that we understand repentance is not a work we do to earn salvation. No one can repent and come to God unless God pulls that person to Him (*John 6:44*). *Acts 5:31* and *11:18* indicate that repentance is something God gives, it is only possible because of His grace. No one can repent unless God grants repentance. All of salvation, including repentance and faith, is a result of God's drawing us, opening our eyes, and changing our hearts. God's longsuffering leads us to repentance (*2 Peter 3:9*), as does His kindness (*Romans 2:4*).

While repentance is not a work that earns salvation, repentance unto salvation does result in works. It is impossible to truly and fully change your mind without that causing a change in action. In the Bible, repentance results in a change in behavior. That is why John the Baptist called people to *"produce fruit in keeping with repentance"* (*Matthew 3:8*). A person who has truly repented from rejection of Christ to faith in Christ will give evidence of a changed life (*2 Corinthians 5:17; Galatians 5:19-23; James 2:14-26*). Repentance, properly defined, is necessary for salvation. Biblical repentance is changing your mind about Jesus Christ and turning to God in faith for salvation (*Acts 3:19*). Turning from sin is not the definition of repentance, but it is one of the results of genuine, faith-based repentance towards the Lord Jesus Christ.

Question: "What is Lordship salvation?"

Lordship Salvation emphasizes that submitting to Christ as Lord over your life goes hand-in-hand with trusting in Christ to be saved. It also focuses on a changed life as the result of salvation. Those who believe in Lordship Salvation would have serious doubts about a person who claims to believe in Christ but does not have good works evident in his life. The Bible does teach that faith in Christ will result in a changed life (*2 Corinthians 5:17; Galatians 5:22-23; James 2:14-26*).

However, depending on the person and his circumstances, spiritual growth sometimes occurs quickly, and other times it takes a long time for changes to become evident, and even then the changes may not be evident to everyone. The Bible clearly teaches that salvation is by faith alone, apart from works (*John 3:16; Ephesians 2:8-9*). The Bible also declares that a life changes after salvation (*Ephesians 2:10*). So it is a difficult balance to make. We do know, however, that we are not to judge another as to the state of his/her eternal soul (*Matthew 7:1*). Only God knows who are His sheep and He will mature each of us according to His perfect time table.

So, is Lordship Salvation Biblical? Again, it cannot be denied that faith in Christ produces a change (*2 Corinthians 5:17*). A person who has been delivered from sin by faith in Christ should not desire to remain in a life of sin (*Romans 6:2*). At the same time, submitting to the Lordship of Jesus Christ is an issue of spiritual growth, not salvation. The Christian life is a process of submitting to God in increasing measure (*2 Peter 1:5-8*). A person does not have to submit to God in every area of his or her life in order to be saved. A person simply has to recognize that he or she is a sinner, in need of Jesus Christ for salvation, and place trust in Him (*John 3:16; Ephesians 2:8-9*). Jesus is Lord (*Philippians 2:10*). Christians absolutely should submit to Him (*James 4:7*). A changed life and submission to Christ's lordship are the result of salvation, not a requirement for salvation.

Question: "How and to whom did Jesus pay our ransom?"

A ransom is something that is paid to provide for the release of someone who is held captive. Jesus paid our ransom to free us from sin, death, and hell. Throughout the books of Exodus, Leviticus, Numbers, and Deuteronomy are found God's requirements for sacrifices. In Old Testament times, God commanded the Israelites to make animal sacrifices for substitutionary atonement; that is, an animal's death took the place of a person's death, death being the penalty for sin (*Romans 6:23*). *Exodus 29:36a* states, *"Each day you must sacrifice a young bull as an offering for the atonement of sin."*

God demands holiness (*1 Peter 1:15-16*). God's Law demands holiness. We cannot give God full holiness because of the sins we commit (*Romans 3:23*); therefore, God demands satisfaction of His Law. Sacrifices to Him satisfied the requirements. This is where Jesus comes in. *Hebrews 9:12-15* tells us *"Once for all time he took blood into that Most Holy Place, but not the blood of goats and calves. He took his own blood, and with it he secured our salvation forever. Under the old system, the blood of goats and bulls and the ashes of a young cow could cleanse people's bodies from ritual defilement. Just think how much more the blood of Christ will purify our hearts from deeds that lead to death so that we can worship the living God. For by the power of the eternal Spirit, Christ offered himself to God as a perfect sacrifice for our sins. That is why he is the one who mediates the new covenant between God and people, so that all who are invited can receive the eternal inheritance God has promised them. For Christ died to set them free from the penalty of the sins they had committed under that first covenant."*

Also, read *Romans 8:3-4, "The law of Moses could not save us, because of our sinful nature. But God put into effect a different plan to save us. He sent his own Son in a human body like ours, except that ours are sinful. God destroyed sin's control over us by giving his Son as a sacrifice for our sins. He did this so that the requirement of the law would be fully accomplished for us who no longer follow our sinful nature but instead follow the Spirit."* Clearly, Jesus paid the ransom for our lives to God. That ransom was His own life, the shedding of His own blood, a sacrifice. Due to His sacrificial death, each person on earth has the opportunity to accept that gift of atonement and be forgiven by God. For without His death, God's Law would still need to be satisfied, by our own death.

Question: "What is the Book of Life?"

Revelation 20:15 declares, *"If anyone's name was not found written in the book of life, he was thrown into the lake of fire."* The Book of Life is the set of names of those who will live with God forever in heaven. It is the roll of those who are saved. This Book of Life is also mentioned in *Revelation 3:5; 20:12*; and *Philippians 4:3*. The same book is also called the Lamb's Book of Life because it contains the names of those who have been redeemed by the blood of the Lord Jesus (*Revelation 13:8; 21:27*).

How do you get your name written in the Book of Life? Simply by repenting of sin and believing in the Lord Jesus Christ as your Savior from sin (*Philippians 4:3; Revelation 3:5*). The moment you place your faith in Jesus as your Savior (*John 3:16; Romans 10:9-10*), your name is written in the Book of Life, never to be erased (*Revelation 3:5; Romans 8:37-39*). No true believer should doubt his eternal security in Christ (*John 10:28-30*).

The Great White Throne Judgment described in *Revelation 20:11-15* is a judgment for unbelievers. That passage makes it clear that no one at that judgment has his name in the Book of Life (*Revelation 20:12-14*). Since their names are not in the Book of Life, their fate is sealed, their punishment is sure.

Some people point to *Revelation 3:5* as "proof" that a person can lose his salvation. However, the promise of *Revelation 3:5* is clearly that the Lord will not erase a name: *"He who overcomes . . . I will not blot out his name from the Book of Life."* An overcomer is one who is victorious over the temptations, trials, and evils of this world. In other words, one who is redeemed. The saved are written in God's registry and have the promise of eternal security.

Another passage over which confusion sometimes arises is *Psalm 69:28*: *"Let them [David's enemies] be blotted out of the book of the living."* This "book of the living" should not be confused with the Lamb's Book of Life. David is referring to earthly, physical life, not eternal life in heaven. The same is true of the "book" mentioned in *Exodus 32:32-33*.

God keeps good records. He knows His own, and He has set the names of His children permanently in His book.

Question: "What does John 3:16 mean?"

We often see signs and banners at sporting events that say *"John 3:16."* Wrongly so, *John 3:16* is often written as graffiti on highway overpasses. Some "entertainers" have thrown in a twist and replaced *"John"* with "something else 3:16." So, what is the big deal with *John 3:16*? Why is this one verse so important?

No other verse in the Bible so succinctly summarizes God's relationship with humanity and the way of salvation. Some consider *John 3:16* as the "theme verse" for the entire Bible. *John 3:16* tells us of the love God has for us and the extent of that love. So great that He sacrificed His only Son on our behalf. *John 3:16* teaches us that anyone who believes in Jesus Christ, God's Son, will be saved. *John 3:16* gives us the glorious hope of eternal life in heaven through the love of God and death of Jesus Christ.

There is no more powerful way to deliver this message than to let *John 3:16* speak for itself. Here is *John 3:16* in 22 different English Bible translations. The words may be slightly different, but the glorious message is the same.

- **New International Version** - *John 3:16, "For God so loved the world that he gave his one and only Son, that whoever believes in him shall not perish but have eternal life."*
- **King James Version** - *John 3:16, "For God so loved the world, that he gave his only begotten Son, that whosoever believeth in him should not perish, but have everlasting life."*
- **New King James Version** - *John 3:16, "For God so loved the world that He gave His only begotten Son, that whoever believes in Him should not perish but have everlasting life."*
- **New American Standard Bible** - *John 3:16, "For God so loved the world, that He gave His only begotten Son, that whoever believes in Him shall not perish, but have eternal life."*
- **The Living Bible** - *John 3:16, "For God loved the world so much that he gave his only Son so that anyone who believes in him shall not perish but have eternal life."*
- **New Living Translation** - *John 3:16, "For God so loved the world that he gave his only Son, so that everyone who believes in him will not perish but have eternal life."*
- **Holman Christian Standard Bible** - *John 3:16, "For God loved the world in this way: He gave His One and Only Son, so that*

everyone who believes in Him will not perish but have eternal life.

- **English Standard Version -** *John 3:16, "For God so loved the world, that he gave his only Son, that whoever believes in him should not perish but have eternal life."*
- **Revised Standard Version -** *John 3:16, "For God so loved the world that he gave his only Son, that whoever believes in him should not perish but have eternal life."*
- **New Revised Standard Version -** *John 3:16, "For God so loved the world that He gave His only Son, so that everyone who believes in Him may not perish but have eternal life."*
- **New International Readers Version -** *John 3:16, "God loved the world so much that He gave His one and only Son. Anyone who believes in Him will not die but have eternal life."*
- **The Message -** *John 3:16, "This is how much God loved the world: He gave His Son, His one and only Son. And this is why: so that no one need be destroyed; by believing in Him, anyone can have a whole and lasting life."*
- **New Century Version a.k.a. International Children's Bible -** *John 3:16, "God loved the world so much that He gave His one and only Son so that whoever believes in Him may not be lost, but have eternal life."*
- **God's Word Translation -** *John 3:16, "God loved the world this way: He gave His only Son so that everyone who believes in Him will not die but will have eternal life."*
- **Contemporary English Version -** *John 3:16, "God loved the people of this world so much that He gave His only Son, so that everyone who has faith in Him will have eternal life and never really die."*
- **New English Bible and Revised English Bible -** *John 3:16, "God loved the world so much that He gave His only Son, that everyone who has faith in Him may not die but have eternal life."*
- **Good News Bible a.k.a. Today's English Version -** *John 3:16, "For God loved the world so much, that he gave His only Son, so that everyone who believes in Him, may not die but have eternal life."*
- **New Jerusalem Bible -** *John 3:16, "Yes, God loved the world so much, that he gave his only Son, so that everyone who believes in him, may not die but have eternal life."*
- **Amplified Bible -** *John 3:16, "For God so greatly loved (dearly prized) the world that He (even) gave up His only begotten (unique) Son, so that whoever believes in (trusts, clings to, relies on) Him shall not perish (come to destruction, be lost) but have*

eternal (everlasting) life."

- **New American Bible -** *John 3:16, "For God so loved the world that He gave His only Son, so that everyone who believes in Him might not perish but might have eternal life."*
- **New English Translation -** *John 3:16, "For this is the way God loved the world: he gave his one and only Son that everyone who believes in him should not perish but have eternal life."*
- **Literal Translation of the Bible -** *John 3:16, "For God so loved the world that He gave His only begotten Son, that everyone believing into Him should not perish, but have everlasting life."*

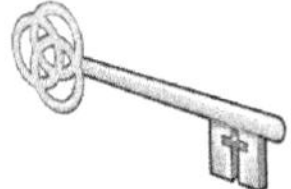

Question: "Is there any sin that God will not forgive?"

For the born-again child of God, there is no unforgivable sin. All sin was forgiven at the cross. When Christ Jesus said *"It is finished"* (*John 19:30*) that statement meant that the penalty for all sin was paid in full. The word translated "it is finished" is the Greek word "tetelestai." That word was used in several ways. It was used to stamp "paid" upon a receipt, and it was also the stamp put on a criminal's charges once he had completed his sentence. A "tetelestai" was nailed to the door of his house proving that he had indeed paid in full for his crimes.

You can see the application to the Cross transaction between the Lord Jesus and God the Father. Jesus Christ completed the legal transaction and satisfied God's holy and righteous demand as the payment for the sin of "*whosoever will.*" The Lord Jesus Christ became our sin sacrifice and "*the Lamb of God who takes away the sin of the world*" (*John 1:29*). When Christ was separated from God the Father for those three hours of supernatural darkness (*Matthew 27:45*), the deal was sealed. As we read in *Luke*, Jesus was reunited with the Father. "*And when Jesus had cried with a loud voice, he said, Father, into thy hands I commend my spirit: and having said thus, he gave up the ghost*" (*Luke 23:46*). Therefore, all sin was paid for once for all.

However, there is a condition upon God's forgiveness of sin. Man must come to God through the Lord Jesus Christ alone. "*Jesus said to him, 'I am the way, the truth, and the life. No one comes to the Father except through Me'"* (*John 14:6*). God's forgiveness is available to all who will come (*John 3:16*), but for those who will not believe upon the Lord Jesus Christ, there is no forgiveness or remission of sin (*Acts 10:43*). Therefore, the only sins God will not forgive in this age of grace are the sins of those who die without first placing their faith in Jesus Christ. By that I mean that a person goes through his life here on this earth and fails to avail himself of the provision that God has provided through the Lord Jesus Christ and goes out into eternity separated from God, and therefore unforgiven.

Born-again believers also sin, and when we do, we put ourselves outside of fellowship with the Lord. However, God has made a provision for that. The Holy Spirit that indwells every born-again believer convicts us and convinces us that we have sinned, and when that happens we have a choice to respond in the right way and renew our fellowship. Once a person is born again and has accepted Christ as his Savior and received remission of sin, there is no way he can lose his eternal life based upon his actions. We can lose our fellowship with God and the joy of our salvation, but that is something we can remedy through confession.

The first epistle of John is a letter written to born-again believers, and it has very practical information on how to walk in fellowship. "*If we confess our sins, he is faithful and just to forgive us our sins, and to cleanse us from all unrighteousness*" (*1 John 1:9*). This verse, when used correctly, becomes the way to restore our fellowship when we sin, and we will. "*If we say that we have no sin, we deceive ourselves, and the truth is not in us*" (*1 John 1:8*). Now, remember, this is a letter to born-again believers. God has no illusions about us and our capacity to sin, and we should not either.

The "if" at the beginning of both 1 John 1:8 and 9 is a third-class "if" in the Greek, and it means "maybe yes, maybe no." There is a condition here; if we "confess." This word in the Greek is "homologia," and it means to say the same thing or cite the case. "Homo" is "same," and "logia" is "word." It means we agree with God that we have sinned. But all sin was forgiven at the Cross and, as born-again believers, all of our sin has been forgiven. And because that is a judicial fact, we need to walk in light and in fellowship because that is our position in Christ Jesus. "*But if we walk in the light as He is in the light, we have fellowship with one another, and the blood of Jesus Christ His Son cleanses us from all sin.*" (*1 John 1:7*). That does not give us carte blanche to continue sinning; rather, a born-again believer who is walking in the light and fellowship of God will be quick to use confession so that there remains a continual and clear fellowship with the Lord on a daily basis.

Question: "Do we contribute anything to our own salvation?"

There are two ways to look at this question, from a practical point of view and a biblical point of view. First, from practical point of view, let's assume that a person does contribute something to his salvation. If that were possible, who would get the credit in heaven? If man somehow contributes to his own salvation, it would follow that man himself gets the credit. And if man gets the credit, this certainly will detract from God's getting the credit. If it were possible to contribute something to attain heaven, then each person upon his arrival would be patting himself on the back because of what he did in order to obtain heavenly citizenship. These same people would be singing, "Praise myself, I contributed to my own salvation." It is unthinkable that people in heaven will be worshiping self rather than God. God said, "*I will not give my glory to another*" (*Isaiah 42:8; 42:11*).

From a biblical point of view, mankind contributes nothing at all to his salvation. The problem with humanity is their sinfulness. Theologians normally refer to this as "total depravity." Total depravity is the belief that mankind is sinful throughout and can do nothing of himself to earn God's favor. Because of this sinful state, mankind wants nothing to do with God, see especially *Romans 1:18-32*. It is safe to say that because mankind is totally depraved, mankind chooses to sin, loves to sin, defends sin, and glories in sin.

Because of man's sinful predicament, he is in need of God's direct intervention. This intervention has been provided by Jesus Christ, the mediator between sinful humanity and righteous God (*1 Timothy 2:5*). As already stated, mankind wants nothing to do with God, but God wants everything to do with man. This is why He sent his son Jesus Christ to die for the sins of humanity, God's perfect substitution (*1 Timothy 2:6*). Because Jesus died, through faith mankind can be declared justified, declared righteous (*Romans 5:1*). By faith, the person is redeemed, bought out of the slave market of sin, and set free from it (*1 Peter 1:18-19*).

Substitution, justification, redemption; these are just a few acts that are provided for completely by God, and devoid completely of anything human. The Bible is clear that mankind cannot contribute anything to his salvation. Any time someone thinks he can contribute, he is in essence working for his salvation, which is clearly against the Bible's statements , see *Ephesians 2:8-9*. Even faith itself is a gift from God. Salvation is a free gift from God (*Romans 6:23*), and since it is a gift, there is nothing you can do to earn it. All you have to do is take the gift. *"But to all who have received him* (i.e., Jesus) *those who believe in his name, he has given the right to become God's children*" (*John 1:12*).

Question: "Is a backsliding Christian still saved?"

This is a question that has been debated endlessly over the years. The word "backslider" or "backsliding" does not appear in the New Testament and is used in the Old Testament primarily of Israel. The Jews, though they were God's chosen people, continually turned their backs on Him and rebelled against His Word (*Jeremiah 8:9*). That is why they were forced to make sacrifices for sin over and over in order to restore their relationship with the God they had offended. The Christian, however, has availed himself of the perfect, once-and-for-all sacrifice of Christ and needs no further sacrifice for his sin. God himself has obtained our salvation for us (*2 Corinthians 5:21*) and because we are saved by Him, a true Christian cannot fall away so as not to return.

Christians do sin (*1 John 1:8*), but the Christian life is not to be identified by a life of sin. Believers are a new creation (*2 Corinthians 5:17*). We have the Holy Spirit in us producing good fruit (*Galatians 5:22-23*). A Christian life should be a changed life. Christians are forgiven no matter how many times they sin, but at the same time Christians should live a progressively more holy life as they grow closer to Christ. We should have serious doubts about a person who claims to be a believer yet lives a life that says otherwise. Yes, a true Christian who falls back into sin is still saved, but at the same time a person who lives a life controlled by sin is not truly a Christian.

What about a person who denies Christ? The Bible tells us that if a person denies Christ, he never truly knew Christ to begin with. *1 John 2:19* declares, *"They went out from us, but they did not really belong to us. For if they had belonged to us, they would have remained with us; but their going showed that none of them belonged to us."* A person who rejects Christ and turns his back on faith is demonstrating that he never belonged to Christ. Those who belong to Christ remain with Christ. Those who renounce their faith never had it to begin with. *2 Timothy 2:11-13, "Here is a trustworthy saying: If we died with him, we will also live with him; if we endure, we will also reign with him. If we disown him, he will also disown us; if we are faithless, he will remain faithful, for he cannot disown himself."*

Question: "How do I get right with God?"

In order to get "right" with God, we must first understand what is "wrong." The answer is sin. *"There is none that doeth good, no, not one"* (*Psalm 14:3*). We have rebelled against God's commands; we have *"like sheep gone astray"* (*Isaiah 53:6*).

The bad news is that the penalty for sin is death. *"The soul that sinneth, it shall die"* (*Ezekiel 18:4*). The good news is that a loving God has pursued us in order to bring us salvation. Jesus declared His purpose was "*to seek and to save that which was lost*" (*Luke 19:10*), and He pronounced His purpose accomplished when He died on the cross with the words *"It is finished!"* (*John 19:30*).

Having a right relationship with God begins with acknowledging your sin. Next come a humble confession of the sin to God (*Isaiah 57:15*) and a determination to forsake the sin. *"With the mouth confession is made unto salvation"* (*Romans 10:10*). This repentance must be accompanied by faith. Specifically, faith that Jesus' sacrificial death, and miraculous resurrection, qualify Him to be your Savior. *"If thou shalt confess with thy mouth the Lord Jesus, and shalt believe in thine heart that God hath raised Him from the dead, thou shalt be saved"* (*Romans 10:9*). Many other passages speak of the necessity of faith, such as *John 20:27; Acts 16:31; Galatians 2:16; 3:11, 26*; and *Ephesians 2:8*.

Being right with God is a matter of your response to what God has done on your behalf. He sent the Savior, He provided the sacrifice to take away your sin (*John 1:29*), and He offers you the promise: "*whosoever shall call on the name of the Lord shall be saved*" (*Acts 2:21*).

A beautiful illustration of repentance and forgiveness is the parable of the prodigal son (*Luke 15:11-32*). The younger son wasted his father's gift in shameful sin (*verse 13*). When he acknowledged his wrongdoing, he decided to return home (*verse 18*). He assumed he would no longer be considered a son (*verse 19*), but he was wrong. The father loved the returned rebel as much as ever (*verse 20*). All was forgiven, and a celebration ensued (*verse 24*).

God is good to keep His promises, including the promise to forgive. "*The Lord is nigh unto them that are of a broken heart, and saveth such as be of a contrite spirit*" (*Psalm 34:18*).

If you want to get right with God, here is a sample prayer. Remember, saying this prayer or any other prayer will not save you. It is only trusting in Christ that can save you from sin. This prayer is simply a way to express to God your faith in Him and thank Him for providing for your salvation. "God, I know that I have sinned against you and am deserving of punishment. But Jesus Christ took the punishment that I deserve so that through faith in Him I could be forgiven. I place my trust in You for salvation. Thank You for Your wonderful grace and forgiveness - the gift of eternal life! Amen!"

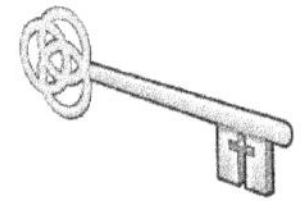

Question: "What is the meaning of Christian redemption?"

Everyone is in need of redemption. Our natural condition was characterized by guilt: "*all have sinned and come short of the glory of God.*"

Christ's redemption has freed us from guilt: "*being justified freely by His grace through the redemption that is in Christ Jesus*" (*Romans 3:23-24*).

The benefits of redemption include eternal life (*Revelation 5:9-10*), forgiveness of sins (*Ephesians 1:7*), righteousness (*Romans 5:17*), freedom from the law's curse (*Galatians 3:13*), adoption into God's family (*Galatians 4:5*), deliverance from sin's bondage (*Titus 2:14; 1 Peter 1:14-18*), peace with God (*Colossians 1:18-20*), and the indwelling of the Holy Spirit (*1 Corinthians 6:19-20*). To be redeemed, then, is to be forgiven, holy, justified, blessed, free, adopted, and reconciled. See also *Psalm 130:7-8; Luke 2:38*; and *Acts 20:28*.

The word redeem means "to buy out." The term was used specifically in reference to the purchase of a slave's freedom. The application of this term to Christ's death on the cross is quite telling. If we are "redeemed," then our prior condition was one of slavery. God has purchased our freedom, and we are no longer in bondage to sin or to the Old Testament law. This metaphorical use of redemption is the teaching of *Galatians 3:13* and *4:5*. Related to the Christian concept of redemption is the word ransom. Jesus paid the price for our release from sin (*Matthew 20:28; 1 Timothy 2:6*). His death was in exchange for our life. In fact, scripture is quite clear that redemption is only possible *"through His blood"* (that is, by His death), *Colossians 1:14*.

The streets of heaven will be filled with former captives who, through no merit of their own, find themselves forgiven and free. The slaves to sin are become saints. No wonder they sing a new song—a song of praise to the Redeemer who was slain (*Revelation 5:9*). We were slaves to sin, condemned to eternal separation from God. Jesus paid the price to redeem us, resulting in our freedom from slavery to sin, and our rescue from the eternal consequences of that sin.

Question: "What is Christian reconciliation? Why do we need to be reconciled with God?"

Imagine two friends who have a fight or argument. The good relationship they once enjoyed is strained to the point of breaking. They cease speaking to each other; communication is deemed too awkward. The friends gradually become strangers. Such estrangement can only be reversed by reconciliation. To be reconciled is to be restored to friendship or harmony. When old friends resolve their differences and restore their relationship, reconciliation has occurred. *2 Corinthians 5:18-19* declares, "*All this is from God, who reconciled us to Himself through Christ and gave us the ministry of reconciliation: that God was reconciling the world to Himself in Christ, not counting men's sins against them. And He has committed to us the message of reconciliation.*"

The Bible says that Christ reconciled us to God (*Romans 5:10; 2 Corinthians 5:18; Colossians 1:20-21*). The fact that we needed reconciliation means that our relationship with God was broken. Since God is holy, we were the ones to blame. Our sin alienated us from Him. *Romans 5:10* says that we were the enemies of God: "*if, when we were enemies, we were reconciled to God by the death of His Son, much more, being reconciled, we shall be saved by His life.*"

When Christ died on the cross, He satisfied God's judgment and made it possible for God's enemies to find peace with Him. Our "reconciliation" to God, then, involves the exercise of His grace and the forgiveness of our sin. The result of Jesus' sacrifice is that our relation has changed from enmity to friendship. "*Henceforth I call you not servants . . . but I have called you friends*" (*John 15:15*). Christian reconciliation is a glorious truth! We were God's enemies, but are now His friends. We were in a state of condemnation because of our sins, but we are now forgiven. We were at war with God, but now have the peace that transcends all understanding (*Philippians 4:7*). "*Therefore, since we have been justified through faith, we have peace with God through our Lord Jesus Christ*" (*Romans 5:1*).

Question: "What is the substitutionary atonement?"

The "substitutionary atonement" refers to the fact that Jesus Christ died on behalf of all sinners. The Scriptures teach that all men are sinners (read *Romans 3:9-18* and *Romans 3:23*). The penalty for our sinfulness is death. *Romans 6:23* reads, "*For the wages of sin is death, but the free gift of God is eternal life in Christ Jesus our Lord.*"

That verse teaches us several things. We are all going to die and spend an eternity in hell as payment for our sins. Death in the scriptures refers to a "separation." Everyone, of course, will die, but some will live in heaven with the Lord for eternity, while others will live a life in hell for eternity. The death spoken of here refers to the life in hell. However, the second thing this verse teaches us is that eternal life is available through Jesus Christ. This is His substitutionary atonement.

Jesus Christ died in our place when He was crucified on the cross. We deserved to be the ones placed on that cross to die because we are the ones who live sinful lives. But Christ took the punishment on His own self in our place. "*He made Him who knew no sin to be sin on our behalf, so that we might become the righteousness of God in Him*" (*2 Corinthians 5:21*). He took our place as a substitute for what we rightly deserved.

"*And He Himself bore our sins in His body on the cross, so that we might die to sin and live to righteousness; for by His wounds you were healed*" (*1 Peter 2:24*). Here again we see that Christ took the sins we committed onto Himself to pay the price for us. A few verses later we read, "*For Christ also died for sins once for all, the just for the unjust, so that He might bring us to God, having been put to death in the flesh, but made alive in the spirit*" (*1 Peter 3:18*). Not only do these verses teach us about the "substitute" that Christ was for us, but also that He was the "atonement," meaning He satisfied the payment due for the sinfulness of man.

One more passage that talks about the "substitutionary atonement" is *Isaiah 53:5*. This verse talks about the coming Christ who was to die on the cross for our sins; it is very detailed, and the crucifixion happened just as it was foretold. Notice the words as you read it. "*But HE was pierced through for OUR transgressions, HE was crushed for OUR iniquities. The chastening for OUR well-being fell upon HIM, and by HIS scourging WE are healed.*" Notice the substitution. Here again we see Christ paid the price for us!

We could not pay the price of sin on our own. Or if we did, we would simply be punished and placed in hell for all eternity. But Christ took the initiative to come to earth in the form of God's Son, Jesus Christ, to pay for the price of our sins. Because He did this for us, we may now have the opportunity to not only have our sins forgiven, but the opportunity to spend an eternity with Him. In order to do this, we must place our faith in what Christ did on the cross. We cannot save ourselves; we need a substitute to take our place.

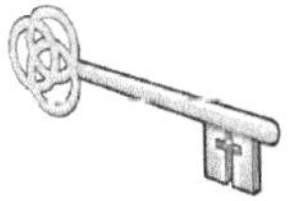

Question: "What is propitiation?"

The word propitiation carries the basic idea of appeasement, or satisfaction, specifically towards God. Propitiation is a two-part act that involves appeasing the wrath of an offended person and being reconciled to him.

The necessity of appeasing God is something many religions have in common. In ancient pagan religions, as well as in many religions today, the idea is taught that man appeases God by offering various gifts or sacrifices. However, the Bible teaches that God Himself has provided the only means through which His wrath can be appeased and sinful man can be reconciled to Him. In the New Testament, the act of propitiation always refers to the work of God and not the sacrifices or gifts offered by man. The reason for this is that man is totally incapable of satisfying God's justice except by spending eternity in hell. There is no service, sacrifice or gift that man can offer that will appease the holy wrath of God or satisfy His perfect justice. The only satisfaction, or propitiation, that could be acceptable to God and that could reconcile man to Him, had to be made by God. For this reason God the Son, Jesus Christ, came into the world in human flesh to be the perfect sacrifice for sin and make atonement or "*propitiation for the sins of the people*" (*Hebrews 2:17*).

The word propitiation is used in several key verses to explain what Jesus accomplished through His death on the cross. For example, in *Romans 3:24-25* we see that believers in Christ have been "*justified freely by His grace through the redemption that is in Christ Jesus, whom God set forth as a propitiation by His blood, through faith, to demonstrate His righteousness, because in His forbearance God had passed over the sins that were previously committed.*" These verses are a key point in Paul's argument in the Book of Romans and are really at the heart of the Gospel message.

In the first three chapters of Romans, Paul has made the argument that everybody, both Jew and Gentile alike, is under the condemnation of God and deserving of His wrath (*Romans 1:18*). Everyone has sinned and fallen short of the glory of God (*Romans 3:23*). All of us deserve His wrath and punishment. God in His infinite grace and mercy has provided a way that His wrath can be appeased and we can be reconciled to Him. That way is through the sacrificial death of His Son, Jesus Christ, as the atonement or payment for sins. It is through faith in Jesus Christ as God's perfect sacrifice, foretold in the Old Testament and fulfilled in the New Testament, that we can be reconciled to God. It is only because of Christ's perfect life, His death on the cross, and His resurrection on the third day that a lost sinner deserving of hell can be reconciled to a Holy God. The wonderful truth of the Gospel message is that Christians are saved from God's wrath and reconciled to God not because "*we loved God, but that He loved us and sent His Son to be the propitiation for our sins*" (*1 John 4:10*).

Jesus said, "*I am the way, the truth, and the life. No one comes to the Father except through Me*" (*John 14:6*). The only way for God's wrath against sinful man to be appeased and for us to be reconciled to God is through Jesus Christ. There is no other way. This truth is also communicated in *1 John 2:2*; "*And He Himself is the propitiation for our sins, and not for ours only but also for the whole world.*" An important part of Christ's saving work includes deliverance from God's wrath that the unbelieving sinner is under, because Jesus' atonement on the cross is the only thing that can turn away God's divine wrath. Those that reject Christ as their Savior and refuse to believe in Him have no hope of salvation. They can only look forward to facing the wrath of God that they have stored up for the coming day of judgment *(Romans 2:5*). There is no other propitiation or sacrifice that can be made for their sins.

Question: "What is justification?"

Simply put, to justify is to declare righteous; to make one right with God. Justification is God declaring those who receive Christ to be righteous, based on Christ's righteousness being imputed to the accounts of those who receive Christ.

Though justification as a principle is found throughout Scripture, the main passage describing justification in relation to believers is *Romans 3:21-26*: "*But now God has shown us a different way of being right in his sight - not by obeying the law but by the way promised in the Scriptures long ago. We are made right in God's sight when we trust in Jesus Christ to take away our sins. And we all can be saved in this same way, no matter who we are or what we have done. For all have sinned; all fall short of God's glorious standard. Yet now God in his gracious kindness declares us not guilty. He has done this through Christ Jesus, who has freed us by taking away our sins. For God sent Jesus to take the punishment for our sins and to satisfy God's anger against us. We are made right with God when we believe that Jesus shed his blood, sacrificing his life for us. God was being entirely fair and just when he did not punish those who sinned in former times. And he is entirely fair and just in this present time when he declares sinners to be right in his sight because they believe in Jesus.*"

We are justified, declared righteous, at the moment of our salvation. Justification does not make us righteous, but rather pronounces our righteousness. Our righteousness comes from placing our faith in the finished work of Jesus Christ. His sacrifice covers our sin, allowing God to see us as perfect and unblemished. Because as believers we are in Christ, God sees Christ's own righteousness when He looks at us. This meets God's demands for perfection; thus, He declares us righteous. He justifies us.

Romans 5:18-19 sums it up well: "*Yes, Adam's one sin brought condemnation upon everyone, but Christ's one act of righteousness makes all people right in God's sight and gives them life. Because one person disobeyed God, many people became sinners. But because one other person obeyed God, many people will be made right in God's sight.*" Why is this pronouncement of righteousness so important? "*Therefore, since we have been made right in God's sight by faith, we have peace with God because of what Jesus Christ our Lord has done for us*" (*Romans 5:1*). It is because of justification that the peace of God can rule in our lives. It is because of the FACT of justification that believers can have assurance of salvation. It is the FACT of justification that enables God to begin the process of sanctification – the process of God making us in reality, what we already are positionally.

Question: "What is regeneration according to the Bible?"

Another word for regeneration is rebirth, from which we get the phrase "born again." To be born again is opposed to, and distinguished from, our first birth, when we were conceived in sin. The new birth is a spiritual, holy, and heavenly birth signified by a being made alive in a spiritual sense. Our first birth, on the other hand, was one of spiritual death because of inherited sin. Man in his natural state is "dead in trespasses and sins" until we are "made alive" (regenerated) by Christ when we place our faith in Him (*Ephesians 2:1*). After regeneration, we begin to see, and hear, and seek after divine things, and to live a life of faith and holiness. Now Christ is formed in the hearts; we are now partakers of the divine nature, having been made new creatures. God, not man, is the source of this (*Ephesians 2:1, 8*). It is not by men's works, but by God's own good will and pleasure. His great love and free gift, His rich grace and abundant mercy, are the cause of it and these attributes of God are displayed in the regeneration and conversion of sinners.

Regeneration is part of the "salvation package," if you will, along with sealing (*Ephesians 1:14*), adoption (*Galatians 4:5*), reconciliation (*2 Corinthians 5:18-20*), and many other salvation concepts. Being born again or born from above is parallel to regeneration (*John 3:6-7; Ephesians 2:1; 1 Peter 1:23; John 1:13; 1 John 3:9; 4:7; 5:1, 4, 18*). Simply put, regeneration is God making a person spiritually alive, a new creation, as a result of faith in Jesus Christ. The reason regeneration is necessary is that prior to salvation we are not God's children (*John 1:12-13*); rather, we are children of wrath (*Ephesians 2:3; Romans 5:18-20*). Before salvation, we are degenerate. After salvation we are regenerated. The result of regeneration is peace with God (*Romans 5:1*), new life (*Titus 3:5; 2 Corinthians 5:17*), and eternal sonship (*John 1:12-13; Galatians 3:26*). This regeneration is eternal and begins the process of sanctification wherein we become the people God intended for us to be (*Romans 8:28-30*).

The Bible is clear that the only means of regeneration is by faith in the finished work of Christ on the cross. No amount of good works or keeping of the law can regenerate the heart which from birth is "*deceitful and wicked above all things*" (*Jeremiah 17:9*). This concept of the new birth is unique to Christianity. No other religion offers a cure for the total depravity of the human heart, preferring instead to outline an often massive body of works and deeds that must be done to gain favor with God. God has told us, though, that "*by works of the law no human being will be justified in his sight*" (*Romans 3:20*). Total regeneration of the heart is necessary for salvation. Paul explains this concept perfectly in *Galatians 2:20*: "*I have been crucified with Christ. It is no longer I who live, but Christ who lives in me. And the life I now live in the flesh I live by faith in the Son of God, who loved me and gave himself for me.*" This is true regeneration.

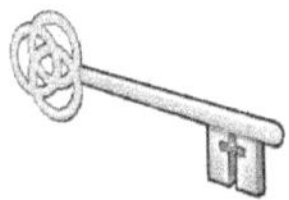

Question: "What is the Ordo Salutis?"

"Ordo Salutis" is the Latin for "the order of salvation" which deals with the steps or stages in the salvation of a believer. These being election, foreknowledge, predestination, redemption, regeneration, justification, sanctification and glorification; see especially *Romans 8:29-30*. There is disagreement within the Church concerning this order, and about the causal connections between them. Before discussion, it might be helpful to provide some basic definitions of many of the terms involved:

- **Foreknowledge:** In this sense, God's knowing prior to salvation those who would be saved.
- **Predestination:** God's choosing before time all who would be saved.
- **Election:** God's choosing of all who would be saved.
- **Regeneration:** God's renewing of one's life, not physically, but as opposed to the spiritual death caused by sin (*Titus 3:5*).
- **Evangelism:** The communication of the Gospel by which one can be saved (*Matthew 28:19*).
- **Faith:** Belief and trust in the message of the Gospel (*Ephesians 2:8-9*).
- **Conversion:** One's turning to God based on the Gospel (*Acts 26:18*).
- **Perseverance:** One's continued true belief - remaining in the state of salvation (*Jude 1:24*).
- **Repentance:** Changing one's mind from rejection of Christ to faith in Christ (*Acts 26:20*).
- **Justification:** God's freeing of one from the penalty of sin; the pronouncement of "not guilty" on a sinner (*Romans 5:9*).
- **Sanctification:** God's separation of one from the lure of sin (*2*

Timothy 2:21).

- **Glorification:** God's final removal of all sin from the life and presence of one (in the eternal state) (*Romans 8:18; 2 Corinthians 4:17*).

The debate over "ordo salutis" is most keenly developed between the Reformed and Arminian systems. For the Reformed tradition, the "ordo salutis" is election / predestination, followed by evangelism, regeneration, conversion, justification, sanctification, and glorification. For the Arminian camp, the "ordo salutis" is evangelism, followed by faith / election, repentance, regeneration, justification, perseverance, and glorification. These stages may have various distinctions that are not represented here, but serve to show the basic differences between the two systems. It should be noted that these need not be conceived as chronological steps. Many of these stages are seen as distinctions within a single process; and each in one way or another, depend upon the work of God.

It is important to realize that the differences are much more than mere labels. One's "ordo salutis" has as much to do with salvation stages as it does with the cause(s) of salvation itself. For example, the Reformed position has faith as an effect of election rather than a cause of it (as the Arminians have it). Thus, there is a sense in which a person is saved in order to have faith. Where, then, should blame be laid if a person does not believe? The Arminian position has the believer responsible for whether or not God saves him, and thus a person must persevere to the end before he can be assured of salvation. What does this say about a believer's security? These and many other questions are dependent upon the "ordo salutis" for their answers, and it is thus important that a believer understands from which perspective those answers are given.

Question: "What does the Bible say about a death bed conversion?"

The most high-profile death bed / last-minute conversion to Christ in the Bible is the case of the criminal crucified alongside Jesus (*Luke*

24:39-43). Only moments before his own death, this criminal had been an unbelieving mocker of Christ (*Matthew 27:44*). However, at the last moment the criminal repented and acknowledged Jesus as the heavenly King. The Lord gave him the blessed promise, "*Today you shall be with Me in Paradise.*"

Although the story of the criminal on the cross demonstrates that last-minute conversions are possible, the Bible warns us to repent now, without waiting another moment. John the Baptist warned, "*Repent, for the kingdom of heaven is at hand*" (*Matthew 3:2*). Jesus had the identical message concerning the need for immediate repentance, "*Repent, for the kingdom of heaven is at hand*" (*Matthew 4:17*).

The Bible warns us concerning the brevity of the human lifespan. "*You are just a vapor that appears for a little while and then vanishes away*" (*James 4:14*). We are not instructed to consider converting someday, but to believe today! "*Today if you hear his voice, do not harden your hearts*" (*Hebrews 3:7-8, 14; 4:7*). None of us knows how much time we have left in this life or what the circumstances of our death will be. We may die in a sudden, unexpected manner that will preclude a deathbed conversion. The only reasonable option is to repent and believe in Jesus Christ today.

Many people die without having the experience of an extended amount of time on a death bed. Many people die instantly and unexpectedly, with no opportunity to trust in Christ. *2 Corinthians 6:2* declares, "*In the time of my favor I heard you, and in the day of salvation I helped you. I tell you, now is the time of God's favor, now is the day of salvation.*"

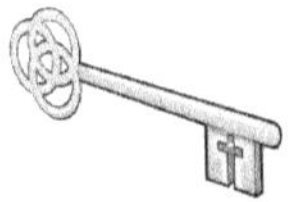

Question: "What are the four spiritual laws?"

The Four Spiritual Laws are a way of sharing the good news of the salvation that is available through faith in Jesus Christ. It is a simple way of organizing the important information in the Gospel into four points.

The first of the Four Spiritual Laws is, "*God loves you and has a wonderful plan for your life.*" *John 3:16* tells us, "*For God so loved the world that He gave His one and only Son, that whoever believes in Him shall not perish but have eternal life.*" *John 10:10* gives us the reason that Jesus came, "*I have come that they may have life, and have it to the full.*" What is blocking us from God's love? What is preventing us from having an abundant life?

The second of the Four Spiritual Laws is, "*Humanity is tainted by sin and is therefore separated from God. As a result, we cannot know God's wonderful plan for our lives.*" *Romans 3:23* affirms this information, "*for all have sinned and fall short of the glory of God.*" *Romans 6:23* gives us the consequences of sin, "*the wages of sin is death.*" God created us to have fellowship with Him. However, humanity brought sin into the world, and is therefore separated from God. We have ruined the relationship with Him that God intended us to have. What is the solution?

The third of the Four Spiritual Laws is, "*Jesus Christ is God's only provision for our sin. Through Jesus Christ, we can have our sins forgiven and restore a right relationship with God.*" *Romans 5:8* tells us, "*But God demonstrates His own love for us in this: While we were still sinners, Christ died for us.*" *1 Corinthians 15:3-4* informs us of what we need to know and believe in order to be saved, "*...that Christ died for our sins according to the Scriptures, that He was buried, that He was raised on the third day according to the Scriptures...*" Jesus Himself declares that He is the only way of salvation in *John 14:6*, "*I am the way and the truth and the life. No one comes to the Father except through me.*" How can I receive this wonderful gift of salvation?

The Fourth of the Four Spiritual Laws is, "*We must place our faith in Jesus Christ as Savior in order to receive the gift of salvation and know God's wonderful plan for our lives.*" *John 1:12* describes this for us, "*Yet to all who received Him, to those who believed in His name, He gave the right to become children of God.*" *Acts 16:31* says it very clearly, "*Believe in the Lord Jesus, and you will be saved!*" We can be saved by grace alone, through faith alone, in Jesus Christ alone (*Ephesians 2:8-9*).

If you want to trust in Jesus Christ as your Savior, say the following words to God. Saying these words will not save you, but trusting in Christ will! This prayer is simply a way to express to God your faith in

Him and thank Him for providing for your salvation. "God, I know that I have sinned against you and deserve punishment. But Jesus Christ took the punishment that I deserve so that through faith in Him I could be forgiven. I place my trust in You for salvation. Thank You for Your wonderful grace and forgiveness - the gift of eternal life! Amen!"

Question: "If our salvation is eternally secure, why does the Bible warn so strongly against apostasy?"

The reason the Bible warns us so strongly against apostasy is that true conversion is measured by visible fruit. When John the Baptist was baptizing people in the Jordan River, he warned those who thought they were righteous to "*bear fruits in keeping with repentance*" (*Matthew 3:7*). Jesus warned those who were listening to Him while He was giving the Sermon on the Mount that every tree can be known by its fruit (*Matthew 7:16*) and that every tree that does not bear good fruit will be cut down and thrown into the fire (*Matthew 7:19*).

The purpose behind these warnings is to counter what some people would call "easy-believism." In other words, following Jesus is more than saying you are a Christian. Anyone can claim Christ as Savior, but those who are truly saved will bear visible fruit. Now, one may ask the question, "What is meant by fruit?" The clearest example of Christian fruit can be found in *Galatians 5:22-23* where Paul describes the fruit of the [Holy] Spirit: love, joy, peace, patience, kindness, goodness, faithfulness, gentleness, and self-control. There are other types of Christian fruit (such as praise, winning souls for Christ), but this list provides us with a good summary of Christian attitudes. True believers will manifest these attitudes in their lives to an increasing degree as they progress in their Christian walk (*2 Peter 1:5-8*).

It is these true, fruit-bearing disciples who have the guarantee of eternal security, and they will persevere to the end. There are many Scriptures that bear this out. *Romans 8:29-30* outlines the "Golden Chain" of salvation by pointing out that those who were foreknown by God were predestined, called, justified, and glorified; there is no loss along the way. *Philippians 1:6* tells us that the work God began in us, He will also finish. *Ephesians 1:13-14* teaches that God has sealed us with the Holy Spirit as a guarantee of our inheritance until we possess it. *John 10:29* affirms that no one is able to take God's sheep out of His hand. There are many other Scriptures that say the same thing; true believers are eternally secure in their salvation.

The passages warning against apostasy serve two primary purposes. First, they exhort true believers to make sure of their "*calling and election.*" Paul tells us in *2 Corinthians 13:5* to examine ourselves to see whether we are in the faith. If true believers are fruit-bearing followers of Jesus Christ, then we should be able to see the evidence of salvation. Christians bear fruit in varying degrees based on their level of obedience and their spiritual gifts, but all Christians bear fruit; and we should see the evidence of that upon self-examination.

Now there will be periods in a Christian's life where there is no visible fruit. These would be times of sin and disobedience. What happens during these times of prolonged disobedience is that God removes from us the assurance of our salvation. Note He doesn't remove our salvation, but the assurance of it. That is why David prayed in *Psalm 51* to restore to him the "*joy of salvation*" (*Psalm 51:12*). We lose the joy of our salvation when we live in sin. That is why we must examine ourselves. When a true Christian examines himself and sees no recent fruitfulness, it should lead to serious repentance and a returning to God.

The second primary reason for the passages on apostasy is to point out apostates. An apostate is someone who abandons his religious faith. It is clear from the Bible that apostates are people who made professions of faith in Jesus Christ, but never genuinely received Him as Savior. *Matthew 13:1-9* (the Parable of the Sower) illustrates this point perfectly. In that parable, a sower sows seed onto four types of soil: hard soil, rocky soil, weed-choked soil, and freshly tilled soil. These soils represent four types of responses to the gospel. The first one is pure rejection, whereas the other three represent various levels of acceptance. The rocky soil and the weed-choked soil represent people who initially respond favorably to the gospel, but when persecution comes (rocky soil) or the cares of the world bear down (weed-choked soil), that person turns away. Jesus makes it clear with these two types of responses that though they initially accepted they never bore any fruit. Again, Jesus says in the Sermon on the Mount, "*Not everyone who says, 'Lord, Lord,' will enter the kingdom*" (*Matthew 7:21*).

It may seem unusual for the Bible to warn against apostasy, and at the same time to say that a true believer will never apostatize. However, this is what Scripture says. *1 John 2:19* specifically states that those who apostatize are demonstrating that they were not true believers. The Biblical warnings against apostasy, therefore, must be a warning to those who are "in the faith" without ever truly having received it. Scriptures such as *Hebrews 6:4-6* and *Hebrews 10:26-29* are warnings to "pretend" believers, that they need to examine themselves and realize that if they are considering apostatizing, they are not truly saved. *Matthew 7:22-23* indicates that those "pretend believers" whom God rejects are rejected not because of having lost faith, but because of the fact that God never knew them.

There are many people who are willing to identify with Jesus. Who doesn't want eternal life and blessing? However, Jesus warns us to count the cost of discipleship (*Luke 9:23-26, 14:25-33*). True believers have counted those costs, whereas apostates have not. Apostates are people who, when they leave the faith, give evidence they were never saved in the first place (*1 John 2:19*). Apostasy is not a loss of salvation, but rather a demonstration that salvation was never truly possessed.

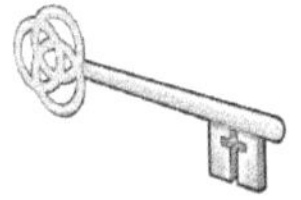

Question: "Why do the four Gospels seem to present a different message of salvation than the rest of the New Testament?"

We must keep in mind that the Bible is intended to be taken as a whole. The books preceding the Four Gospels are anticipatory, and the books which follow are explanatory. Throughout the whole Bible, what God requires is faith; *Genesis 15:6, Psalm 2:12, Habakkuk 2:4, Matthew 9:28, John 20:27, Ephesians 2:8, Hebrews 10:39.* Salvation comes not by our own works but by trusting what God does on our behalf.

Each of the Gospels has its own emphasis on the ministry of Christ. Matthew, writing to a Jewish audience, emphasizes Jesus' fulfillment of Old Testament prophecy, proving that He is the long-awaited Messiah. Mark writes a fast-paced, condensed account, recording Jesus' miraculous deeds and not recording His long discourses. Luke portrays Jesus as the remedy of the world's ills, emphasizing His perfect humanity and humane concern for the weak, the suffering, and the outcast. John emphasizes Jesus' deity by selecting many conversations and sayings of Jesus on the subject and also including "signs" that prove He is the Son of God.

The Four Gospels work together to provide a complete testimony of Jesus, a beautiful portrait of the God-Man. Although the Gospels differ slightly in theme, the central Subject is the same. All present Jesus as the One who died to save sinners. All record His resurrection. Whether the writers presented Jesus as the King, the Servant, the Son of Man, or the Son of God, they had the common goal; that people believe in Him.

We'll delve into the theology of the Gospels now. John includes many statements of faith and commands to believe. These inclusions fit his stated purpose, *"that you might believe that Jesus is the Christ, the Son of God; and that believing you might have life through His name"* (*20:31*). The other Gospels (the Synoptics) are no less concerned that we trust in Christ. Their appeals to faith are less overt but are just as genuine.

Jesus proclaims the need for righteousness, and He warns of the penalty of sin, which is hell. However, Jesus always presents God as the standard of righteousness and Himself as the means of righteousness; without Christ righteousness is unattainable and hell is inevitable. The Sermon on the Mount (*Matthew 5-7*) is a case in point:

- Jesus begins the Sermon on the Mount with a description of the blessed life (*5:1-12*). The Beatitudes are not telling us "how to" be righteous, but are simply describing righteousness.
- He presents Himself as the fulfillment of the Old Testament law (*5:17-18*). This is a key verse because, to earn our own righteousness, we must fulfill the law; here, Jesus says that He will do it for us.
- He says that no amount of our own good works will gain us entrance to heaven (*5:20*). This is another important statement in the sermon. The Pharisees were the most religious people of the day, but Jesus says even they are not good enough to enter heaven. Jesus will go on to say that it's not a religious system that saves, but He Himself.

- He “raises the bar” for righteousness according to God’s standard, instead of man’s interpretation of the law (*5:21-48*). He explains God’s intent behind seven Old Testament laws. The bar is raised so high as to make everyone, even the most dedicated religious practitioner, guilty before God.
- He describes three popular religious activities almsgiving, prayer, and fasting as hypocritical when practiced by the outwardly religious (*6:1-18*). Jesus’ focus, as with the seven laws He just mentioned, is the heart condition of man, not the works we can see.
- He warns that there will be “many” in the day of judgment who will have performed great works for God yet will be turned away from heaven (*7:21-23*). The reason given is that Jesus never “knew” them. There was no familial relationship, only “good” works, which is not enough.
- Jesus concludes the Sermon on the Mount with the audacious statement that He alone is the foundation for building one’s religious life (*7:24-27*). It is an appeal to trust “*these sayings of Mine*” enough to abandon all other foundations.

To summarize, in the Sermon on the Mount Jesus meticulously deconstructs the pharisaical religion of good works, points to a holiness greater than our own, and offers Himself as the sole basis of religion. Accepting what Jesus says in this sermon requires faith in His Person.

Matthew’s Gospel goes on to emphasize faith in the following verses:

- *8:10, 13, 26;*
- *9:2, 22, 28-29;*
- *12:21;*
- *13:58;*
- *14:31;*
- *15:28;*
- *16:8;*
- *17:17;*
- and *18:6.*

Also, Matthew includes a very clear presentation of Jesus as the Son of God in this exchange: “*He said to them, ‘But who do you say that I am?’ Simon Peter answered and said, ‘You are the Christ, the Son of the living God.’ Jesus answered and said to him, ‘Blessed are you, Simon Bar-Jonah, for flesh and blood has not revealed this to you, but My Father who is in heaven.’*” (*Matthew 16:15-17*).

Mark's Gospel contains the following references to faith in Christ:

- *1:15;*
- *2:5;*
- *4:40;*
- *5:34, 36;*
- *6:6; 9:19, 23, 42;*
- *10:52;*
- *11:23;*
- and *16:14.*

In Luke's Gospel we see these verses promoting faith in Christ:

- 1:1;
- 5:20;
- 7:9, 50;
- 8:12, 25, 48, 50;
- 9:41;
- 12:28, 46;
- 17:19;
- 18:8, 42;
- and 24:25.

As we continue to see scripture as a unified whole, we will see that there is only one message of salvation, and the Four Gospels provide the basis for that message.

The Epistles which follow the Gospels elaborate upon the same theme: salvation by faith in Christ. The overarching theme of Romans is the righteousness that comes through God and the doctrine of justification by grace through faith. The central theme of Galatians and Colossians is the same. The book of Hebrews stresses the pre-eminence and perfection of Christ, the "author and perfecter of our faith." First & Second Corinthians, Ephesians, Philippians, First & Second Thessalonians, the pastoral epistles of Timothy & Titus, Philemon, James, and First & Second Peter all describe the holy living, both personally and corporately within the church, and the hope for the future which should be the natural result of life in Christ. The three epistles of John reiterate the basics of the faith and warn against those who would call them into question, which is also the main theme of Jude. Revelation, the final book of the New Testament, presents the last act of God's plan for mankind and the fate of those who hold onto the same faith expounded in the entirety of the New Testament - faith in Christ alone.

Question: "Can a person be saved through general revelation?"

General revelation can be defined as "the revelation of God to all people, at all times, and in all places, that reveals that God exists and that He is intelligent, powerful, and transcendent." Scriptures such as *Psalm 19:1-4* and *Romans 1:20* clearly state that certain things about God can be understood from nature and the universe around us. For more information, please read our article on the differences between general revelation and special revelation. In regards to the question, "Can a person be saved through general revelation?" This question is usually asked in relation to another question, "What happens to those who have never heard the Gospel?"

Sadly, there are still parts of the world with absolutely no access to the Bible, to the Gospel of Jesus Christ, or to any means of learning Christian truth. The question then arises, what happens to these people when they die? Is it fair for God to condemn a person who has never even heard the Gospel, nor heard of Jesus Christ, nor even heard that there is a God? Some propose a solution to this dilemma in the idea that God judges those who have never heard based on how they responded to general revelation. The presumption is that if a person truly believes what can be known about God through general revelation, God will judge the person based on that faith and allow the person entrance into Heaven. Is it possible that such a concept is true?

Before we address that question, a key assumption must be dealt with. Some make the assumption that those who have never heard the Gospel are searching for God, seeking for truth, practically begging for someone to come and deliver the message of salvation. The problem with this assumption is that Scripture declares the exact opposite. *Romans 3:10-12* exclaims, *"There is no one righteous, not even one; there is no one who understands, no one who seeks God. All have turned away, they have together become worthless; there is no one who does good, not even one."* According to Scripture, people take the knowledge of God available through general revelation and pervert it to their own liking. *Romans 1:21-23* states, *"For although they knew God, they neither glorified Him as God nor gave thanks to Him, but their thinking became futile and their foolish hearts were darkened. Although they claimed to be wise, they became fools and exchanged the glory of the immortal God for images made to look like mortal man and birds and animals and reptiles."* According to Scripture, the "status" of those without God is not one of seeking salvation, but rather one of rebellion, darkness, and idolatry.

Back to the question at hand, can a person be saved through general revelation? The Bible nowhere gives any hope that those who have never heard the Gospel are fully believing the truth about God available through general revelation. Again, the Bible describes the lost as being in rebellion against what they already know about God, not seeking for more truth about God. However, there is always the question, "What if?" IF a person who has never heard the Gospel truly and fully believed what can be known about God through general revelation, would that person be saved? IF such a person did exist, it would seem consistent with the love, mercy, and grace of God that such a person would be saved. Again, please understand, this is a hypothetical that Scripture does not support.

Acts chapter 10 records the story of Cornelius. Cornelius is described as *"devout and God-fearing; he gave generously to those in need and prayed to God regularly"* (*Acts 10:2*). Did God save Cornelius because of his devotion to God based on the limited knowledge he had of God? No. God sent an angel to Cornelius with instructions for Cornelius to contact the Apostle Peter and have him come to Cornelius' home. Cornelius obeyed, and Peter came and presented the Gospel to Cornelius and his family. Cornelius and his family believed and were therefore saved (*Acts 10:44-48*). *Acts chapter 10* is a clear example of how we are not saved by believing certain truths about God, or by obeying God in certain respects. The only way of salvation is the Gospel of Jesus Christ (*John 14:6; Acts 4:12*).

The fact that the lost reject general revelation is the reason why it is so important for us to proclaim the Gospel throughout the whole world (*Matthew 28:19-20; Acts 1:8*). *Romans 10:14* declares, *"How, then, can they call on the one they have not believed in? And how can they believe in the one of whom they have not heard? And how can they hear without someone preaching to them?"* God commands us to present the Gospel because of the fact that *"there is no one righteous, not even one; there is no one who understands, no one who seeks God"* (*Romans 3:10-11*). Rather than hoping some people are being saved by believing what can be known about God through general revelation, God calls us to go into all the world and proclaim the Gospel. Believing in the Gospel of salvation through Jesus Christ is the only method of salvation the Bible mentions (*John 3:16*)

Question: "What does it mean for salvation to be a gift from God?"

The word gift is an important one in the Bible, and it is good that we understand its definition and implications.

In the New Testament, there are several Greek words translated "gift." Some of these words are used in contexts other than God's gift of salvation, such as the reciprocal gift-giving of celebrants (*Revelation 11:10*), the things received from fathers (*Matthew 7:11*), offerings to a ministry (*Philippians 4:17*), and the gifts of the magi (*Matthew 2:11*).

However, when it comes to the matter of our salvation, the New Testament writers use different Greek words, words that emphasize the gracious and absolutely free quality of the gift. Here are the two words most commonly used for the gift of salvation:

- **Dorea** - a free gift. This word lays particular stress on the gratuitous nature of the gift, it is something given above and beyond what is expected or deserved. Every New Testament occurrence of this word is related to a spiritual gift from God. It is what Jesus offers to the Samaritan woman at the well (*John 4:10*). It is called the *"free gift"* in *Romans 5:15*. It is the *"unspeakable [or indescribable] gift"* in *2 Corinthians 9:15*. This gracious gift is identified as the Holy Spirit in *Acts 2:38; 8:30* and *11:17*. The adverb form of this word is **dorean**, translated *"freely"* in *Matthew 10:8; 2 Corinthians 11:7*; and *Revelation 21:6; 22:17*. In *Romans 3:24*, immediately following God's pronouncement of our guilt, we have this use of **dorean**: *"Being justified FREELY by His grace, through the redemption that is in Christ Jesus."* The gift of salvation is free, and the motive for the gift is nothing more than the grace of the Giver.
- **Charisma** - a gift of grace. This word is used to define salvation in *Romans 5:15-16* and also, in *Romans 6:23*: *"For the wages of sin is death, but the GIFT [charisma] of God is eternal life through Jesus Christ our Lord."* This same word is used in conjunction with the gifts of the Spirit received after salvation (*Romans 12:6; 1 Timothy 4:14; 2 Timothy 1:6; 1 Peter 4:10*). Obviously, if something is a "gift of grace," it cannot be earned. To work for something is to deserve it, and that would produce an obligation; a gift of debt, as it were. That is why works destroy grace (*Romans 4:1-5; 11:5-6*).

When presenting salvation, the New Testament writers carefully chose words that emphasize grace and freedom. As a result, the Bible could not be more clear; salvation is absolutely free, the true gift of God in Christ, and our only responsibility is to receive the gift by faith (*John 1:12; 3:16; Ephesians 2:8-9*).

Question: "How can salvation be not of works when faith is required? Isn't believing a work?"

Our salvation depends solely upon Jesus Christ. He is our substitute, taking sin's penalty (*2 Corinthians 5:21*); He is our Savior from sin (*John 1:29*); He is the author and finisher of our faith (*Hebrews 12:2*). The work necessary to provide salvation was fully accomplished by Jesus Himself, who lived a perfect life, took God's judgment for sin, and rose again from the dead (*Hebrews 10:12*).

The Bible is quite clear that our own works do not help merit salvation. *"Not by works of righteousness which we have done"* (*Titus 3:5*). *"Not of works"* (*Ephesians 2:9*). *"There is none righteous, no not one"* (*Romans 3:10*). This means that offering sacrifices, keeping the commandments, going to church, being baptized, and other good deeds are incapable of saving anyone. No matter how "good" we are, we can never measure up to God's standard of holiness (*Romans 3:23; Matthew 19:17; Isaiah 64:6*).

The Bible is just as clear that salvation is conditional; God does not save everyone. The one condition for salvation is faith in Jesus Christ. Nearly 200 times in the New Testament, faith (or belief) is declared to be the sole condition for salvation (*John 1:12; Acts 16:31*).

One day, some people asked Jesus what they could do to please God: *"What shall we do, that we might work the works of God?"* Jesus immediately points them to faith: *"This is the work of God, that ye believe on Him whom He hath sent"* (*John 6:28-29*). So, the question is about God's requirements (plural), and Jesus' answer is, *"God's requirement (singular) is that you BELIEVE Me."*

Grace is God's giving us something we cannot earn or deserve. According to *Romans 11:6*, "work" of any kind destroys grace. The idea is that a worker earns payment, while the recipient of grace simply receives it, unearned. Since salvation is all from grace, it cannot be earned. Faith, therefore, cannot truly be considered a "work," or else it would destroy grace. See also *Romans 4*, Abraham's salvation was dependent on faith in God, as opposed to any work he performed.

Suppose an unknown benefactor, someone with whom I had no previous dealings whatsoever, sent me a check for $1,000,000. The money is mine if I want it, but I still must endorse the check. In no way can signing my name be considered earning the million dollars, the endorsement is a non-work. I can never boast about becoming a millionaire through sheer effort or my own business savvy. No, the million dollars was simply a gift and signing my name was the only way to receive it. Similarly, exercising faith is only the way to receive the generous gift of God, and faith cannot be considered a work worthy of the gift.

True faith cannot be considered a work because true faith involves a cessation of our works in the flesh. True faith has as its object Jesus and His work on our behalf. See *Matthew 11:28-29* and *Hebrews 4:10.*

To take this a step further, true faith cannot be considered a work because even faith is a gift from God, not something we produce on our own. *"For by grace are ye saved, through faith; and that [faith] not of yourselves: it [faith] is the gift of God"* (*Ephesians 2:8*). *"No man can come to Me, except the Father which hath sent Me draw him"* (*John 6:44*). Praise the Lord for His power to save and for His grace to make salvation a reality!

Question: "How can I become a child of God?"

"But to all who did receive Him [Jesus], who believed in His name, He gave the right to become children of God" (*John 1:12*).

- **"You must be born again"** - When visited by the religious leader, Nicodemus, Jesus did not immediately assure him of heaven. Instead, Christ said, *"Truly, truly, I say to you, unless one is born again he cannot see the kingdom of God"* (*John 3:3*). The first time a person is born, he inherits the sin nature that stems from Adam's disobedience in the Garden of Eden. No one has to teach a child how to sin. He naturally follows his own wrong desires, leading to such sins as lying, stealing, and hating. Rather than being a child of God, he is a child of disobedience and wrath. *"And you were dead in your trespasses and sins, in which you formerly walked according to the course of this world, according to the prince of the power of the air [Satan], of the spirit that is now working in the sons of disobedience. Among them we too all formerly lived in the lusts of our flesh, indulging the desires of the flesh and of the mind, and were by nature children of wrath, even as the rest"* (*Ephesians 2:1-3*). As children of wrath, we deserve to be separated from God in hell. Thankfully, the passage continues, *"But God, being rich in mercy, because of His great love with which He loved us, even when we were dead in our transgressions, made us alive together with Christ (by grace you have been saved)"* (*Ephesians 2:4-5*). How are we made alive with Christ / born again / made a child of God? We must receive Jesus!

- **Receive Jesus -** *"But to all who did receive Him [Jesus], who believed in His name, He gave the right to become children of God"* (*John 1:12*). This passage clearly explains how to become God's child. We must receive Jesus by believing in Him. What must we believe about Jesus?
    - First, we must recognize that Jesus is the eternal Son of God who became man. Born through the power of the Holy Spirit by the virgin Mary, Jesus did not inherit Adam's sin nature. Therefore, He is called the second Adam (*1 Corinthians 15:22*). While Adam's one disobedience brought the curse of sin on the world, Christ's perfect life can cover our sinful ones. Our response must be to repent (turn from sin), trusting His perfect life to purify us.
    - Second, we must have faith in Jesus as Savior. God's plan was to sacrifice His perfect Son on the cross to pay the punishment we deserve for our sin: death. Christ's death frees those who receive Him from the

penalty and power of sin.

  - Finally, we must follow Jesus as Lord. After raising up Christ as the Victor over sin and death, God gave Him all authority (*Ephesians 1:20-23*). Jesus leads all who receive Him; He will judge all who reject Him (*Acts 10:42*).

By God's grace giving us repentance and faith in the Savior and Lord, we're born again to new life as God's child. Only those who receive Jesus; not merely knowing about Him but relying on Him for salvation, submitting to Him as Master and loving Him as the supreme treasure, become God's child.

- **Become a child of God** - *"But to all who did receive Him, who believed in His name, He gave the right to become children of God, who were born, not of blood nor of the will of the flesh nor of the will of man, but of God"* (*John 1:12-13*). Just as we had no part in our natural birth, we cannot cause ourselves to be born into God's family by doing good deeds or conjuring up faith of our own. As the above verses say, God is the one who *"gave the right"* according to His gracious will. *"See how great a love the Father has bestowed on us, that we would be called children of God"* (*1 John 3:1*). Thus, God's child has nothing to be proud about but boasts only in the Lord (*Ephesians 2:8-9*). A child grows up to look like his parents. Similarly, God wants His children to become more and more like Jesus Christ. Although only in heaven will we be perfect, a child of God will not habitually, unrepentantly sin. *"Little children, make sure no one deceives you; the one who practices righteousness is righteous, just as He is righteous; the one who practices sin is of the devil; for the devil has sinned from the beginning. The Son of God appeared for this purpose, to destroy the works of the devil. No one who is born of God practices sin, because His seed abides in him; and he cannot sin, because he is born of God. By this the children of God and the children of the devil are obvious: anyone who does not practice righteousness is not of God, nor the one who does not love his brother"* (*1 John 3:7-10*). Make no mistake; a child of God cannot be "disowned" by sinning. But someone who "practices" sin (i.e. consistently enjoys sin without heed for following Christ and His Word) reveals that he was never born again. Jesus told such people,

> *"You are of your father the devil, and you want to do the desires of your father"* (*John 8:44*). God's children, on the other hand, no longer crave the gratification of sin but desire to know, love, and glorify their Father. The rewards of being God's child are immeasurable. As God's child, we are a part of His family (the church), promised a home in heaven, and given the right to approach God in prayer as Father (*Ephesians 2:19; 1 Peter 1:3-6; Romans 8:15*).

Respond to God's call to repent of sin and believe in Christ. Become God's child today!

Question: "What does the Bible say about household salvation?"

Having a proper understanding of what the Bible teaches concerning household salvation must begin with an understanding of what the Bible teaches about salvation in general and election in particular. To begin with, we know that there is only one way of salvation, and that is through faith in Jesus Christ (*Matthew 7:13-14; John 6:67-68; John 14:6; Acts 4:12; Ephesians 2:8*). We also know that the command to believe is directed to individuals and the act of believing is an individual action. Understanding this is important when it comes to correctly understanding the concept of household salvation because it helps us focus on the fact that salvation can only come through an individual believing in Christ. It is not something that a father can do for a son or daughter, nor is the fact that one member of a family or household believes any guarantee that the rest will also.

In fact, Jesus Himself indicates that the Gospel often divides families. For example, in *Matthew 10:34-36* Jesus said: *"Do not think that I came to bring peace on earth. I did not come to bring peace but a sword. For I have come to 'set a man against his father, a daughter against her mother, and a daughter-in-law against her mother-in-law'; and a man's enemies will be those of his own household."* Also, if we understand what the Bible teaches about election, we again come to understand that God elects individuals to salvation and that only those that are elect will be saved (*John 6:44-65*). This indicates that both election and salvation are not corporate but individual in nature. God elects individuals to salvation (*Romans 9:6-18*), and those that are elect believe and are saved (*Acts 13:48*).

So, if salvation is an individual action, then how are we to understand those passages in the Bible that seem to contain a promise of household salvation? How can we reconcile the need for individuals to believe in order to be saved and the promises of verses like *Acts 11:14* that indicate a promise was given to Cornelius that his household would be saved? First of all, like any passage of Scripture, it is important to understand the genre or type of book the verse is in. In this case it is found in *Acts*, which is an historical narrative of actual events that took place. This is important because the fact that God promised Cornelius that his whole household would be saved does not mean the same promise applies universally to all households across time. In other words, it was a specific promise to a specific person at a specific point in time. One must be very careful about interpreting these types of promises as universal in nature because they must be understood correctly in their historical setting in order to be correctly interpreted.

Second, we need to look at how God fulfilled His promise to Cornelius. If we go back to *Acts 10:33*, we first see that Cornelius and his household were gathered *"to hear all that you (Peter) have been commanded by the Lord."* In other words, they were in a place and position to hear the Gospel which *"is the power of God to salvation"* (*Romans 1:16*). Upon hearing the Gospel preached by Peter, everyone in Cornelius's household believed and was baptized (*Acts 11:15-18*). So, while God had promised Cornelius that his household would be saved, the way they were saved was consistent with God's plan of salvation, which is through the preaching of the Gospel. They were not saved because Cornelius believed but because they believed.

Another passage in Acts that carries the promise of household salvation is found in *Acts 16:31*. Here the Philippian jailer asks, *"Sirs, what must I do to be saved?"* To which Paul and Silas respond, *"Believe in the Lord Jesus, and you shall be saved, you and your household."* Again, it is important to remember that this promise is given to a specific individual in a specific context; however, unlike the promise to Cornelius, this one contains a promise that is clearly universal in nature and spans all time periods and contexts. That promise is not one of household salvation but is one that is entirely consistent with every other verse in the Bible that speaks of salvation. It is the promise that if you believe in the Lord Jesus *"you shall be saved."* Also, if we continue to study this passage in context, we see again that salvation came as the result of hearing the Word of God and responding in faith (*Acts 16:32*). Again, this is consistent with every other verse in the Bible concerning salvation. Individual people hear the gospel and respond in faith and are saved. They were not saved because they were part of the jailer's household; instead, they were saved because they believed the Gospel message and responded in faith.

A third verse in the New Testament that some will use to try to teach household salvation is *1 Corinthians 7:14*: *"For the unbelieving husband is sanctified through his wife, and the unbelieving wife is sanctified through her believing husband; for otherwise your children are unclean, but now they are holy."* Is this verse somehow teaching that an unbelieving spouse can be sanctified or saved on the basis of their spouse's faith in Christ, or that their children will be holy before the Lord because one of their parents is saved? Of course, the obvious answer to that is "no" because that is totally inconsistent with the overall teaching of Scripture. That becomes even clearer when one again examines the context of the passage. In this case, the passage is not dealing with salvation or sanctification (being made holy before God) at all. Instead, it is dealing with the marriage relationship between a husband and wife, and this and the following passages deal specifically with the issue of a Christian who has an unbelieving spouse. Paul taught that Christians should not be *"unequally yoked" (2 Corinthians 6:14*) with unbelievers. Here in this passage, he clarifies that if a believer is already married to an unbeliever they should remain married as long as the unbeliever consents to do so. The reason this would be allowable is that the marriage relationship would be sanctified (holy or set apart in God's eyes) based upon the faith of the believing spouse. Likewise, the children of that marriage will be legitimate in the sight of God despite the fact that Christians are not to be unequally yoked with the lost.

Noted Greek scholar A.T. Robertson in his book *"Word Pictures of the New Testament"* writes this about *1 Corinthians 7:14*: *"Paul does not, of course, mean that the unbelieving husband is saved by the faith of the believing wife. Clearly, he only means that the marriage relation is sanctified so that there is no need of a divorce. If either husband or wife is a believer and the other agrees to remain, the marriage is holy and need not be set aside. ....If the relations of the parents be holy, the child's birth must be holy also (not illegitimate)."*

The fact that *1 Corinthians 7:14* is not speaking of some type of household salvation is clearly seen in the rhetorical question that Paul asks in *1 Corinthians 7:16*: *"For how do you know, O wife, whether you will save your husband? Or how do you know, O husband, whether you will save your wife?"* The obvious answer is they don't because only God knows who will be saved and who will not be.

While there really is no promise of "household salvation" that a believer can lay claim to, that does not mean that we should not earnestly hope, pray, and work for the salvation of our families. And while there are times as foretold by Jesus in *Matthew 10:34-36* that salvation will divide a family, there are also many times where the God of Abraham also becomes the God of Sarah, and then of Isaac and then of Jacob. As Charles Spurgeon said: *"...though grace does not run in the blood, and regeneration is not of blood nor of birth, yet doth it very frequently—I was about to say almost always—happen that God, by means of one of a household, draws the rest to himself. He calls an individual, and then uses him to be a sort of spiritual decoy to bring the rest of the family into the gospel net."* God has not only appointed or elected individuals to salvation. He has also ordained the means by which they will be saved, which is hearing and responding in faith to the Gospel message. As Spurgeon so eloquently communicates, this often involves a family member, as God saves one person and then uses him/her in such a way that others in the family hear the Word of God, believe, and are saved.

Question: "Is it possible for a person's name to be erased from the Book of Life?"

Revelation 22:19 says, *"And if any man shall take away from the words of the book of this prophecy, God shall take away his part out of the book of life, and out of the holy city, and from the things which are written in this book."* This verse is usually involved in two major controversies, the debate about biblical preservation and the debate concerning eternal security. The question we will concern ourselves with is the latter. Does *Revelation 22:19* mean that once a person's name is written in the Lamb's Book of Life, it can at some time in the future be erased? In other words, can a Christian lose his salvation?

First, Scripture is clear that a true believer is kept secure by the power of God, sealed for the day of redemption (*Ephesians 4:30*) and of all those whom the Father has given to the Son, He will lose none of them (*John 6:39*). The Lord Jesus Christ proclaimed, *"I give them eternal life, and they shall never perish; no one can snatch them out of my hand. My Father, who has given them to me, is greater than all; no one can snatch them out of my Father's hand"* (*John 10:28-29b*). If the "anyone" referred to in *Revelation 22:19* are not believers, who are they? In other words, who might want to either add to or take away from the words of the Bible?

Most likely this would be done by those who only profess to be Christians and who suppose that their names are in the book of life. In fact, most of the corruptions of the Scriptures have been attempted by those who have professed some form of Christianity. Generally speaking, the two main groups who have traditionally tampered with the *Revelation* are pseudo-Christian cults and those who hold to very liberal theological beliefs. Many cults and theological liberals claim the name of Christ as their own, but they are not "born again" the definitive biblical term for a Christian.

The Bible cites several examples of those who thought they were believers, but whose profession was proven to be false. In *John 15*, Jesus refers to them as branches that did not remain in Him, the true Vine, and therefore did not produce any fruit. We know they are false because *"by their fruits you shall know them"* (*Matthew 7:16, 20*) and true disciples will always exhibit the fruit of the Holy Spirit who resides within them (*Galatians 5:22*). In *2 Peter 2:22*, Peter likens the false professors to dogs returning to their own vomit and the sow who *"after washing herself returns to wallow in the mire"*. The barren branch, the dog who returns to his own vomit, and the pig that washes herself are all symbols of those who profess to have salvation, but who have nothing more than their own righteousness to rely upon, not the righteousness of Christ which truly saves.

It is doubtful that those who have repented of their sin and been born again would willingly tamper with God's Word in this way; adding to it or taking from it. Of course we recognize that good people have sincerely held differences of opinion and belief in the area of textual criticism! But it CAN be demonstrated how cultists and liberals have repeatedly done both, *"adding to"* and *"taking away from."* Thus, we can understand God's warning as found in *Revelation 22:19* in this manner: Anyone who tampers with this crucial message will find that God did not place their name in the Book of Life, will deny them access to His Holy City, and they will forfeit any expectation of all the good things He promises to His saints in this book.

Finally, from a purely logical standpoint, why would the sovereign and omniscient God; He who knows the end from the beginning (*Isaiah 46:10*), write a name in the Book of Life when He knows He will only have to erase it when that person eventually apostatizes and denies the faith? Additionally, if you read this warning within the context of the paragraph in which it appears, *Revelation 22:6-19,* you can clearly see God remains consistent in His theology: only those who have taken heed of His warnings, repented and been born again, will have any good to look forward to in eternity. All others, sadly, have a terrible and terrifying future awaiting them.

Question: "What is easy believism?"

"Easy believism" is a somewhat derogatory term used by opponents of the view that one needs only to believe in Jesus in order to be saved. From this they conclude that those who hold to sola fide (faith alone) are saying that no corresponding need exists for a committed life of Christian discipleship as proof of salvation, but this is not true. Those who use the term easy believism are confusing justification, the one-time act of being declared righteous by God, with sanctification, the lifelong process by which the justified believer is conformed to the image of Christ. Those who call salvation by faith "easy believism" miss the fact that true conversion will always result in sanctification and a life of good works.

Much of this debate is unnecessary and is based on a misunderstanding of the Scriptures. The Bible is clear that salvation is by grace alone, through faith alone, in Christ alone. The essence of this doctrine is found in *Ephesians 2:8-9*: *"For by grace are you saved, through faith, and that not of yourselves. It is the gift of God, not of works, lest any man should boast."* So we see that faith, given as a gift by God, is what saves us. But the next verse tells of the results of that salvation: *"For we are his workmanship, created in Christ Jesus unto good works, which God hath before ordained that we should walk in them."* Rather than being saved by some easy act of our own wills, we are saved by the hand of God Almighty, by His will and for His use. We are His servants, and from the moment of salvation by faith, we embark on a journey of pre-ordained good works that are the evidence of that salvation. If there is no evidence of growth and good works, we have reason to doubt that salvation ever truly took place. *"Faith without works is dead"* (*James 2:20*), and a dead faith is not a saving faith.

Faith alone does not mean that some believers follow Christ in a life of discipleship, while others do not. The "others" here refers to a separate category of believer known as the "carnal Christian," a completely unscriptural concept. Believers in the idea of the carnal Christian say that a person may receive Christ as Savior during a time of decision or religious experience, but never manifest any evidence of a changed life. This is a false and dangerous teaching. It provides a convenient excuse for the person who does not want to follow Christ. Such a person is lulled into a false sense of security thinking he/she has eternal life. The Bible nowhere supports the idea that a true Christian can remain carnal for an entire lifetime. Rather, God's Word presents only two categories of people, Christians and non-Christians, believers and unbelievers, those who have bowed to the Lordship of Christ and those who have not (*John 3:36; Romans 6:17-18; 2 Corinthians 5:17; Galatians 5:18-24; Ephesians 2:1-5; 1 John 1:5-7; 2:3-4*).

While the security of salvation is a biblical fact based upon the finished work of salvation by Christ, it is certainly true that some of those who seemed to have "made a decision" or "accepted Christ" may not genuinely be saved. As noted before, true salvation is not so much our accepting Christ as it is His accepting us. When we are truly saved, it is by the power of God for the purpose of God, and that purpose includes the works that are the evidence of our conversion. Those who continue to walk according to the flesh are not believers. This is why Paul exhorts us to *"examine yourselves to see whether you are in the faith"* (*2 Corinthians 13:5*). The "carnal" Christian who examines himself will soon see that he/she is not in the faith.

James 2:19 says, *"You believe that there is one God. You do well. Even the demons believe—and tremble!"* The type of "belief" demons have can be compared to the intellectual assent made by those who "believe" in Jesus only in the fact that He exists. Many unbelievers say, "I believe in God," or "I believe in Jesus," or perhaps some might say, "I prayed a prayer and the preacher said I was saved." The problem is in the understanding of the word believe. With true salvation comes genuine repentance and real life change. *Second Corinthians 5:17* tells us that when we are in Christ, we are a "new creation." Is it possible that the new person Christ creates is one who continues to walk in the carnality of the flesh? It is not.

Salvation is certainly free, but at the same time, it costs us everything. We are to die to ourselves as we become more and more changed into the likeness of Christ. Where easy believism fails is in its lack of recognition that a person who has truly believed in Jesus as the Savior will have a progressively changed life. Salvation is a free gift from God to those who believe, but discipleship and obedience are the response and responsibility which will no doubt occur when one truly comes to Christ in faith.

Question: "How are predestination and election connected with foreknowledge?"

Certainly, since God knows everything, it would have been possible for God to base His predestination and election of individuals upon His foreknowledge of the future. In fact, that is the exact position that many Christians believe, as it is the Arminian view of predestination. The problem is that it really is not what the Bible teaches about predestination, election, and foreknowledge. In order to understand why the view that *"God made His choice based on merely knowing the future"* is not what the Bible teaches, let's first consider a couple of verses that speak to the reason God elected or predestined people to salvation.

Ephesians 1:5 tells us that God *"predestined us to be adopted as his sons through Jesus Christ, in accordance with his pleasure and will."* According to this verse, the basis of our being predestined is not something that we do or will do, but is based solely on the will of God for His own pleasure. As *Romans 9:15-16* says, *"I will have mercy on whomever I will have mercy, and I will have compassion on whomever I will have compassion. It does not, therefore, depend on man's desire or effort, but on God's mercy."* Similarly, *Romans 9:11* declares regarding Jacob and Esau, *"Yet, before the twins were born or had done anything good or bad—in order that God's purpose in election might stand: not by works but by him who calls."* Then again in *Ephesians 1:11* we see that people are *"chosen, having been predestined according to the plan of him who works out everything in conformity with the purpose of his will."* From these and many others passages, we see that Scripture consistently teaches that predestination or election is not based upon something that we do or will do. God predestined people based on His own sovereign will to redeem for Himself people from every tribe, tongue, and nation. God predetermined or predestined this from before the foundation of the world (*Ephesians 1:4*) based solely on His sovereign will and not because of anything that He knew the people would do.

But what about *Romans 8:29* where it says that those *"He foreknew, He also predestined"*? Doesn't that seem to say that predestination is based upon the foreknowledge of God? Of course, the answer is yes, it does teach that predestination is based on the foreknowledge of God. But what does the word foreknowledge mean? Does it mean *"based upon God's knowledge of the future,"* meaning God simply looks down through the future and sees who will believe the gospel message and then predestines or elects them? If that were the case, it would contradict the verses above from Romans and Ephesians that make it very clear election is not based on anything man does or will do.

Fortunately, God does not leave us to wonder about this issue. In *John 10:26*, Jesus said, *"But you do not believe because you are not of My sheep."* The reason some people believe is that they belong to God. They were chosen for salvation, not based on the fact that they would one day believe, but because God chose them for *"adoption as sons in Christ Jesus"* before they ever existed. The reason one person believes and another person does not is that one person has been adopted by God and the other has not. The truth is that the word foreknew in *Romans 8:29* is not speaking of God's knowing the future. The word foreknowledge is never used in terms of knowing about future events, times or actions. What it does describe is a predetermined relationship in the knowledge of God whereby God brings the salvation relationship into existence by decreeing it into existence ahead of time.

The word "know" is sometimes used in the Bible to describe an intimate or personal relationship between a man and a woman. In a similar sense, before God ever created the heavens and earth, and a long time before we were ever born, God knew His elect in a personal way and chose them to be His sheep, not because they would someday follow Him but in order to guarantee that they would follow Him. His knowing them and choosing them is the reason they follow Him, not the other way around. The issue really is not whether or not God knows who will believe, but why some believe and others do not. The answer to that is God chooses to have mercy on some and others He leaves in their sinful rebellion.

The following quote by John Murray is excellent in dealing with this issue: *"Even if it were granted that 'foreknew' means the foresight of faith, the biblical doctrine of sovereign election is not thereby eliminated or disproven. For it is certainly true that God foresees faith; He foresees all that comes to pass. The question would then simply be: whence proceeds this faith, which God foresees? And the only biblical answer is that the faith which God foresees is the faith He himself creates (cf. John 3:3-8; 6:44, 45, 65; Eph. 2:8; Phil. 1:29; 2 Peter 1:2). Hence His eternal foresight of faith is preconditioned by His decree to generate this faith in those whom He foresees as believing."*

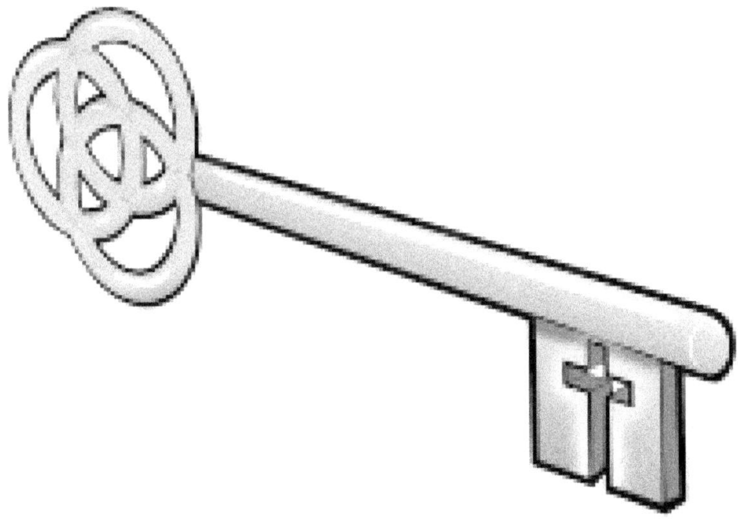

www.ingramcontent.com/pod-product-compliance
Lightning Source LLC
LaVergne TN
LVHW010934110826
845149LV00013B/2596